The Challenge of Islam
to the Church and its Mission

The Challenge of Islam
to the Church and its Mission

Patrick Sookhdeo Ph.D., D.D.

The Challenge of Islam to the Church and its Mission

Published in the United States by Isaac Publishing
6729 Curran Street, McLean VA 22101

ISBN 978-0-9787141-5-4
Printed and bound in the United Kingdom
by Cromwell Press Group Ltd, Trowbridge, Wiltshire

This book is a revised and updated edition of Patrick Sookhdeo's
Islam: the Challenge to the Church (Pewsey: Isaac Publishing, 2006).

Contents

A Personal Note from the Author 2

Preface 6

1 Introduction 10

2 Understanding Islam 18
Basic theology
Social issues
Spirituality, morality and culture
Diversity in Islam
Trends in contemporary Islam

3 Comparing Islam with Christianity 52
Theological understanding of Islam

4 Issues 60
Legal protection
Education
Treatment of women
Implementation of *shari'a*
Media and freedom of speech
Politics
Cruel *shari'a* punishments
Dhimmi
Apostasy
Jihad and the extension of Islamic territory

5 Christian-Muslim Relations 76
Building friendships
Places of worship
Joining in Islamic worship
"Dialogue"
Christian-Muslim cooperation on non-religious projects
Christian-Muslim cooperation on overseas aid, relief and development
Christian-Muslim cooperation on religious projects
Reconciliation
Mission and evangelism
Convert care
Involvement in society
Justice

6 Conclusion **114**

Appendix **118**

Barnabas Fund Response to the Yale Center for Faith and Culture Statement

Differences Between the Muslim and the Christian Concept of Divine Love -
Dr. Murad Wilfried Hofmann

The Concept of Love in Islam - a paper by Barnabas Fund

Glossary **164**

References and Notes **168**

Index of Bible References **178**

Index of Qur'an References **179**

Index of *Hadith* References **181**

Index. **182**

All quotations from the Qur'an in this book have been taken from the widely distributed translation *Interpretation of the Meanings of the Noble Qur'an in the English Language: A Summarized Version of At-Tabari, Al-Qurtabi and Ibn Kathir with comments from Sahih Al-Bukhari Summarized in One Volume,* by Muhammad Taqi-ud-Din Al Hilali and Muhammad Muhsin Khan, 15ᵗʰ revised edition (Riyadh: Darussalam, 1996).

Different translations of the Qur'an can vary slightly in the numbering of the verses. If using another translation it may be necessary to search the verses preceding or following the reference to find the same text.

A Personal Note from the Author

I was born in Guyana, South America in 1947 and lived there until I was 12. Guyana in the 1950s was – and still is – very mixed in terms of ethnicity, culture and religion. There were Muslims, Hindus and Christians, and people of African, Asian and European descent as well as indigenous Amerindians.

But we all lived together in peace and harmony. We ate each other's food and celebrated each other's festivals. No faith sought to gain religious or political dominance. No faith felt threatened or intimidated by another one. No faith was legally advantaged or disadvantaged more than the others. I was brought up in a Muslim family and started being taught the Qur'an at the age of 4½. The imam did not teach us to hate or despise other faiths, or that it was our duty to attack other faiths; he simply taught us to chant the Qur'an.

Now I am a Christian and live in another multiethnic, multicultural and religiously plural society, the UK. I remember in the 1960s how we immigrants did our best to assimilate into the majority culture and to become as British as we could as fast as we could. But nowadays some minorities have a different attitude. I am both grieved and alarmed to see how equality, peace and harmony in British society are fast disappearing, for which the main cause seems to be the egregious behaviour of a radical minority within one particular faith, Islam. There is such fear of radical Islam that few voices dare to point out what is happening.

It does not have to be like this. I **know** that from my personal experience. Hundreds of thousands of other Guyanese of my age will have similar memories. The same inter-religious harmony has also existed in other places at other times. It is possible for faiths to live together in peace without one subjugating the rest.

The Iranian liberal Muslim writer, Amir Taheri, has pointed out how extraordinarily politicized Islam in the West has become, to the point where God is hardly mentioned in sermons. He says that the UK's 2,000 or so mosques are basically "a cover for a political movement", i.e. that British Islam has become "a political movement masquerading as a religion." Taheri suggests three reasons for this. Firstly, Muslims in the West come from a wide variety of backgrounds but are unable to continue here their historic sectarian feuds. So they lay aside theological issues and unite on other issues such as hatred of gay marriages or of Israel. Secondly, Western freedoms have allowed Islamic political movements to flourish, movements which are suppressed or banned in many parts of the Muslim world. Thirdly, there has been a rapprochement between British Islam and the extreme Left, which work together on issues such as anti-war, anti-America and anti-Israel.[1]

We need to guard our liberties, not take them for granted. Although we know that the gates of hell will not ultimately prevail against the Church which the Lord is building, there are sections of his Church which have disappeared completely in the face of the challenge of Islam, for example, North Africa which was once a major centre of Christianity. Christians in Victoria State, Australia, are bitterly regretting that they did not oppose the passing of the Racial and Religious Tolerance Act in 2001 which now stifles their preaching and teaching. "We did not give enough thought to it at the time," some said to me in January 2006.

Another main challenge which Islam presents to the Church is the care of converts. Becoming a Christian was a difficult experience for me, with all its attendant trials and alienation. Being a Christian from a non-Western background is also very difficult, as I have lived through the end of colonialism and have also faced considerable racism from the white Christian community.

It is my hope and prayer that this book will help Christians in the West to think about the issues which surround Islam, so that they will be enabled to respond to the challenge of Islam before it is too late.

Patrick Sookhdeo
McLean VA
April 29, 2008

Preface

Islam is a religion of law, rituals, duties, faith, power and territory. A Muslim's worldview and values are derived from these essential Islamic principles, in just the same way that a Christian's worldview and values are derived from Christian spirituality.

The aim of this book is to help Christians in the West to understand Islam and the challenge which the rise of Islam in the West poses to the Church and its mission. While these challenges affect Christian individuals not only as Christians but also as members of society, this book will mainly focus on the challenge of Islam to the life, work and witness of the Body of Christ.[2]

The book is written from within a Western context of massive loss of confidence among Christians, accompanied by confusion, uncertainty and sometimes even shame. This context is the result of a process which became evident after the end of the Second World War, a process in which individualism, utilitarianism, materialism and hedonism gradually gained prominence and influence. Meanwhile duty, loyalty and even Christianity itself became increasingly scorned. The vacuum left by the virtual demise of Christianity was first filled by secular humanism but latterly Islam is gaining many converts from those with a spiritual hunger who are seeking a faith to follow. The more radical sections of Islam are in turn joining forces with traditionally atheistic movements such as the hard Left who share their anti-globalism, anti-capitalism sentiments and their deep-seated animosity towards Western liberal democracies. A third ally for the Islamism-Extreme Left partnership is found in liberal Christianity.

At the same time there has been an increasing sense of shame amongst some white Westerners, particularly Britons, who have been taught to believe the very worst about the British Empire. They feel they can do no right, and believe that because of the "sins" of earlier generations (such as colonialism and the Crusades) they have forfeited the right even to comment on other people's culture or religion. Thus, in preparation for the 2007 bicentenary of the abolition of the slave trade by the British Parliament, the Church of England, under the guidance of the Archbishop of Canterbury, made a statement apologizing to the descendants of the slave trade's victims, but making no mention at all of the victory of abolition. This all-pervading shame and sense of ineligibility to critique non-Westerners may be one reason why (until recently) very few white Britons offered any criticism of the radical and violent aspects of Islam.

In the United States it is not so much a matter of shame and loss of confidence, as in the UK and parts of Europe, but of increasing political correctness. An entrenched multiculturalism works against the recognition or establishment of any common culture that is too closely related to the history and values of the majority, and especially those rooted in traditional and Judeo-Christian concepts of morality and reason. A further aspect is the way in which black identity has become increasingly merged with a new kind of Islam, which many orthodox Muslims believe to be heretical, i.e. the Nation of Islam.

The accusation of Islamophobia is often leveled against those who draw attention to aspects of Islam which do not meet modern standards of human rights etc. It is important to recognize the distinction between Islam the religious ideology and Muslims the people who follow it. While it is possible and in some situations necessary to draw attention to negative aspects of a religious ideology, the attitude of Christians to Muslims as fellow human beings should always be one of love, compassion and concern.

It is important also to recognize that all faiths, including Christianity, have been misused by their followers at various times and places. We must acknowledge that atrocities and injustices have been perpetrated in the name of Christ, and we must avoid the pitfall of comparing the beautiful ideals of one faith with the less than perfect practices of another.

Although Islam is basically totalitarian in nature and dissent is rarely allowed, paradoxically there is and always has been a wide diversity of opinion within Islam, and numerous mutually intolerant divisions, sects and movements exist. Despite this there is a core orthodoxy which is fairly easy to identify and it is this "standard" Islam which will be our main focus. We will also look briefly at the differences between some of the major groupings and trends within Islam.

Islam is multifaceted in a way that is unlike any other religion. In Islam there is no separation between sacred and secular, or between spiritual and material. Islam encompasses the social, legal, cultural, political and even military aspects of life. Because of this there is a serious problem of understanding with regard to Christians approaching Islam; many of the terms used by the two faiths are identical, giving the impression of a close similarity of thought-processes, and yet the meanings can be radically different.

Christians seeking to enter into dialogue with Muslims need to understand this core orthodoxy and inherent unity within the Islamic faith. Recent years have seen a rise in the phenomenological approach to other religions, which looks for commonalities between different faiths such as holy men, holy places or holy things. This approach does not suit Islam. Focusing on aspects of religious phenomena in Islam which are apparently held in common with Christianity does not lead to a correct understanding of Islam. This book will therefore attempt to look at Islam as a Muslim does, i.e. seeing the whole rather than the separate parts. While examining in turn a multiplicity of issues, each must always be understood in the light of the whole system that is Islam.

We have already considered the importance of distinguishing Islam the religion, which is not only a faith but also seeks political power and territory, from Muslims the followers of that religion. Muslim people are like every other human being on earth, made in the image of God. They are loved by God and must be loved by Christians as well. We are called to love our enemies and pray for those who persecute us (Matthew 5:44). There can be no place for hatred or fear in our relationships with Muslims. Furthermore, as Christians we have a divine mandate to witness to Muslims of the saving work of our Lord Jesus, who died not only for us but also for them. This we do with the love of Christ, for as Paul the apostle wrote, "The love of Christ urges us on, because we are convinced that one has died for all." (2 Corinthians 5:14) It is hoped that this book will not only help in the understanding of Islam the religion but will also act as a spur in our witness to Muslim people who so desperately need the Savior.

Introduction

The tragic events of September 11, 2001 spawned a huge interest in Islam. In the seven years since then Islam has become a frequent topic of debate and analysis in Western media, society and Church. Perhaps it could be said that we have never had so much information in so many areas on Islam and Muslims. Added to this are factors such as the growth of Muslim minorities in the West, the "war on terrorism" (which so far has been largely a war on Islamic terrorism), the American-led incursions into Afghanistan and Iraq, the reactions of the Muslim community worldwide, Iran's proposed nuclear program, and the international Muslim reaction against publication of cartoons of Muhammad, the prophet of Islam. All these issues have brought Islam to center stage and are forcing a radical re-think of Western opinion on the nature of Islam.

Formerly driven chiefly by factors such as post-colonial guilt and sympathy for the perceived underdog, the debate is now fueled by fresh theories such as a revisionist approach to history, by Samuel Huntington's thesis of an inevitable "clash of civilizations" (between Islam and the West), and by a philosophical and linguistic deconstructionism that negates all absolutes.

Interestingly there has also been a dramatic change in Muslim presentations of their faith to outsiders. This phenomenon began before September 11, 2001, but the rate has increased rapidly since that date. The impetus is the desire to defend Islam from any negative criticism and to present it as entirely positive and devoid of anything blameworthy throughout its history. This has been described as "the turbaning of the mind". Muslim governments with their multiplicity of agencies and institutions as well as Muslim communities in the West are determined that their religion be understood and respected and so have launched major movements through television, radio, newspapers, books, articles, internet, lecturers and preachers to educate non-Muslims. Islam appears to aspire literally to rewrite the text-books.

To the efforts of Muslim governments are added those of Western governments who increasingly believe that, in order to avert Islamic violence, they must accord respect to the religion of Islam. They have therefore launched their own movements to educate the non-Muslim public about the nature of Islam. Thus the US governments are seeking to counter the perceived terrorist threat at home and abroad by promoting the concept that Islam is essentially peaceful, like Christianity, but has been subverted and distorted by a small number of violent extremists. Furthermore Western governments have created an interfaith "industry" which they are funding in the belief that through interfaith relations Muslims will become more moderate, violence will be averted, and peace and harmony will result. Interfaith has now become a vehicle not only of the US government but also of other governments' policies.

Churches, first the liberals and now increasingly the evangelicals as well, have followed this lead and taken on the governmental interfaith agenda. Whereas in the 1980s the World Council of Churches was the architect of inter-religious dialogue and propounded an interfaith movement emphasizing the commonality of all religions, now evangelicals are increasingly taking on this mantle.

Of course, it is right and proper for governments, for churches and for individual Christians to work for good community and religious relations and to prevent religiously motivated violence. But where a government is in effect using the Church as its tool to achieve this task, the effect can be very damaging; it associates Christianity with government policy which can have negative effects for Christian minorities in the Muslim world who are held responsible for the acts of Western governments.

Through engagement with Muslims, through inter-religious dialogue, through support for Islamic causes and interests, many Christians of all kinds now seem to believe that they must help to rehabilitate Islam and establish it in the public domain. Together with secular politicians, Christians are emerging as the defender, protector and unifier of Islam. Some do this in the hope that Muslims will reciprocate by respecting Christians and allowing evangelism to occur freely within their countries. Others do it out of fear inasmuch that they believe - as the Muslims would have them believe - that the two religions will soon be involved in a catastrophic war with each other. Thus they seek to avert this war by joining forces with Islam. Still others do it because they have let their emotions guide their intellect and theology; they have generalized from a moderate peaceable Muslim individual whom they know and like and have come to believe that those are the characteristics of the religion as a whole. Such Christians have great difficulties in critiquing Islam because of their love for Muslims in general or their friendship with particular Muslim individuals. Whilst Christians are most certainly called to love Muslims, those who have followed this track of affirming and promoting Islam seem unable to distinguish Islam the theology and ideology from Muslims the people. Such Christians have unwittingly embraced Islam the faith as they sought to embrace Muslims the people. Then there are those Christians who believe that the Church has much to learn from Islam. They emphasize the commonalities between Islam and Christianity, and see Christ's reconciling work as involving the whole of humanity.

Such a plethora of positions on Islam has led to great confusion, and Christians are now deeply divided. Islam has in fact become an agent of division amongst Christians both liberals and evangelicals. Some denominations such as the Roman Catholic Church led by Pope Benedict XVI and the Orthodox denominations have not capitulated to the increasing Islamic demands. Rather they have sought to hold on to their theological foundations. For Protestant Christians, and in particular evangelical Christians, caught up in post-modernity and loosened from their theological moorings, Islam may well prove to be decisive in terms of their own survival. It was Professor Johan Bouman of Marburg, Germany, who observed that Islam could pose a much greater challenge to Christianity in the twenty-first century than Gnosticism did to the early Church.

President Theodore Roosevelt once said, "If I must choose between righteousness and peace, I choose righteousness." For Christians in our day it is important that we choose righteousness, which includes truth and justice, rather than sacrifice them in the uncertain hope of peace with Islam. This principle is true for the Church as well as for nations, as Roosevelt observed.

So what attitude **should** the Christian Church adopt towards this other major world faith, seemingly sharing so much doctrine in common with Christianity and yet clearly so very different in reality? The purpose of this book is to help Christians answer this question. We shall first look at the nature of Islam, and compare it with Christianity. Key contemporary issues will be examined in turn, each one being crucial to the way in which Islam is manifested in contemporary society. Finally, we look at some of the practical issues of Christian-Muslim relations in the West.

Contemporary Islam increasingly focuses on classical Islam and its manifestations. Classical Islam was formulated in the first few centuries after Muhammad, and in the tenth century AD it was agreed that the work had been completed. The consensus (in Sunni Islam, which comprises at least 80% of Muslims today) is that no alteration can now be made to the regulations laid down by the early Islamic scholars. The process by which such change could be made is known as *ijtihad* and this is what both liberal Muslims and Islamists claim to be doing as they seek to reform Islam in their respective directions. However, among the great mass of Muslims in general there is enormous fear of making any alterations to the traditional rulings, as this would be deemed blasphemy or apostasy.

Thus it is effectively impossible to change or adapt Islam. Consequently there is an inevitable conflict between certain aspects of Islam and some modern societal norms. This conflict is far more than just a question of mental anguish for the individual, because a vital part of Islam is living out one's faith in society. Faith, to a Muslim, is not merely personal but has social, political and cultural implications. A typical Muslim believes that their faith must impact the society in which they live and must contribute to the Islamic character of that society. This political aspect appears to have become the dominant feature of Islam in the West. It is only the relatively few liberal Muslims who would consider flouting orthodoxy by trying to adapt their faith to integrate into modern society.

The late Dr Zaki Badawi, who was president of the Muslim College in London, expressed the underlying assumption within Islam that Muslims must live in an Islamic society, ordered according to the teachings of Islam.

> The history of Islam as a faith is also the history of a state and a community of believers living by Divine law. The Muslims, jurists and theologians have always expounded Islam as both a Government and a

faith. This reflects the historical fact that Muslims, from the start, lived under their own law. Muslim theologians naturally produced a theology with this in view – it is a theology of the majority. Being a minority was not seriously considered or even contemplated.[3]

Badawi went on to explain that there is no consensus within Islam about how Muslims should live as a minority within a non-Muslim majority.

Omar Ahmed, the founder of the Council on American Islamic Relations (CAIR), the largest Muslim "civil liberties" group in the United States that works "to promote a positive image of Islam and Muslims in America," believes that Islam must become dominant in the US.

Islam isn't in America to be equal to any other faith, but to become dominant. The Koran, the Muslim book of scripture, should be the highest authority in America, and Islam the only accepted religion on Earth.[4]

Thus Islam is bound to impact the societies in which it finds itself. This impact is felt in six primary areas, as defined by Rev. Albrecht Hauser: spiritual, theological, missiological, societal, political and in the area of justice.

Islam is a spiritual movement, which throughout history has had a strangling effect on the Christian Church. There has been much oppression and suffering, since Islam considers Christians to have gone astray and since Islam rejects and considers the central beliefs of Christians to be obsolete.

Theologically the whole concept of incarnation, the vicarious death of Christ and his redemptive cross is rejected in Islam, so also is the Trinitarian understanding of God. The cross is veiled and the challenge for the Christian Church is to understand and happily confess why Jesus is truly God and truly man. Since Islam believes in the unity of the sacred and secular, and of the state and religion, it also poses a political challenge. Islam needs to be viewed in many ways as an ideology seeking to gain political power. Islam is not only a religion in the Western sense, but also an ideology with a total claim on the society and political life of its adherents, ruled by divine, rather than secular law. Since the divine law *(shari'a)* is considered superior to all man-made laws of secular societies there is always a tendency to push for other legislation to be made to conform to the *shari'a*.[5]

Western Christians who are concerned to react in an appropriate, loving, scriptural and Christ-like way to the presence of Islam in their societies must have a clear understanding of the nature of Islam – its theology, ethics and culture – so as to discern where there is common ground and where there are differences. This will help in the crucial decisions that have to be made on how to approach Muslims, and indeed how to respond to the approaches that they make to Christians. For it must not be forgotten that, while many Christians are seeking a rapprochement with Islam, many Muslims are at the same time seeking to neutralize and negate all forms of Christian mission. Increasingly Muslim countries are seeking the removal of all foreign missionaries and the cessation of missionary activities. National evangelists are being persecuted and threatened, with some being killed. International Islamic agencies are claiming that mission and evangelism are divisive, anti-Islamic and responsible for growing Islamophobia, and therefore must cease.

Furthermore, Muslims are also increasingly active in proselytization themselves. In the spiritual vacuum found in the materialistic twenty-first century West, Muslim missionaries often find their message is welcomed. They are skilled at presenting their faith in a positive light and in persuading the general public that words like *jihad* and *shari'a*, have purely benign meanings. They also make good use of more familiar words like "freedom" and "equality" which actually carry different meanings in Islam but this is not clarified to the non-Muslim audience. They are working not only to make individual converts but also to change the worldview of Western societies as a whole to conform to Islamic beliefs and values. The Church – which should be able to recognize this challenge more easily than society at large can – has a vital role to stand in the gap and help Western society at large to protect its Judeo-Christian heritage and to re-attach itself to its long-forgotten spiritual roots in the Bible, roots which have formed and guided Western society so much more than is usually realized.

Understanding Islam

Basic theology

Definition of Islam

The term "Islam" is defined as follows: "The Arabic word 'Islam' simply means 'submission'... In a religious context it means complete submission to the will of God."[6] Muslims sometimes claim that Islam means peace. It is true that both *salam* (peace) and *islam* (submission) come from the same root. But in Arabic a root can carry a variety of different meanings. The root S-L-M has eight or ten different "measures" or forms, each carrying different meanings, including to touch, to betray, to consent, to be safe. Form 1 leads to the noun *salam* (peace). Form 4 leads to the nouns *islam* (submission) and *Islam* (the religion).

Muhammad's life

Muslims believe that Muhammad was the final prophet, after whom no other prophets will come. All previous prophets were only relevant for their time.

According to Islamic teaching, Muhammad (c. 570 – 632 AD) was an Arabian merchant who at the age of 40 began to receive a series of messages for mankind, which Muslims believe came from the angel Gabriel. (Christians will of course question whether the angel who announced the birth of Christ could 600 years later have brought a message so contrary to the teachings of Christ.) He and his early followers were mocked and persecuted in his home town of Mecca so they began to flee to Medina, with Muhammad himself finally joining them in 622. In Medina Muhammad set up an Islamic state, with himself as judge, ruler and military commander.[7]

The attitude of most Muslims to Muhammad is best described as veneration. This is a paradoxical aspect of Islam, a faith which in theory affirms the believer's direct access to God without the need for any intercessor. Accordingly, Muhammad **should** be viewed by Muslims as simply a human channel for God's revelation. In practice, however, Muhammad's figure towers over Islam not just as its founder, but as the "perfect man" who was divinely inspired not only in his Qur'anic revelations, but in all his sayings and deeds, thus making his life normative for all times. "As a messenger he is the last and greatest, about whom the early messengers have predicted and who thus completes the process of revelation. He is therefore the Perfect Ideal for Mankind, the perfect servant of Allah and hence the most complete and ideally balanced manifestation of the attributes of Allah."[8] He is considered infallible, free from sin, and serves as the supreme example whom all Muslims are obliged to emulate in every small detail.

Muhammad is also seen as the intercessor with God who can change the divine decrees and admit those he intercedes for into paradise. Love for Muhammad (and his family) is strongly instilled into most Muslim children. Many Muslims, especially in the Indian subcontinent, hold that Muhammad was created from an eternal heavenly substance (Muhammadan light) that pre-existed with God. He is a logos-like figure similar to Christ – a sinless mediator and intercessor.

A main concern of Muslims is the person of Muhammad who must be protected from any criticism or slight. Protecting his honor is an obligation on all. Any suspected denigration of Muhammad immediately creates disturbances and riots in many Muslim countries and communities, more so than blasphemy against God himself.

Scriptures

> The Qur'an is a record of the exact words revealed by God through the Angel Gabriel to the Prophet Muhammad. It was memorized by Muhammad and then dictated to his Companions, and written down by scribes, who crosschecked it during his lifetime. Not one word of its 114 chapters, suras, has been changed over the centuries, so that the Qur'an is in every detail the unique and miraculous text which was revealed to Muhammad fourteen centuries ago.[9]

The original is believed by Muslims to be inscribed in Arabic on a tablet in heaven, hence the great reverence accorded to it and to the Arabic language. Islam has a similar concept of revelation to Mormonism.

However, non-Muslim scholars and early Islamic writings have a different understanding of how the Qur'an developed. Early Islamic sources say that it was not written down until after Muhammad's death. It is also clear that there were many versions of the Qur'an in existence for some time, until Caliph Uthman ordered the suppression of all but one version between 650 and 656. However, despite Uthman's efforts (and contrary to what Muslims believe), two versions of the Qur'an remained as late as the mid-twentieth century, the minority version being used by some North African Muslims.

Non-Muslim scholars have also shown how many of the teachings of the Qur'an resemble a distorted version of Christianity and Judaism. Indeed it is not necessary to be much of a scholar to see this. Muhammad would not have required an angelic messenger to provide him with the Qur'an; he could have composed it on the basis of what he learnt from Arab Christians he met, perhaps seeking to correct and purify a faith which he could see the Christians themselves had rather a poor grasp of.

Second in importance to the Qur'an are a collection of traditions about what Muhammad and his earliest followers said and did, known as the *hadith*. The *hadith* are used by Islamic scholars to interpret the Qur'an (which in many places is vague and ambiguous), i.e. to indicate how the Qur'an should be understood and therefore what Muslims should do in any particular situation. The example of Muhammad and the first Muslims provides guidance on areas where the Qur'an is silent or incomprehensible.

Allah (the Arabic term for "God")

The three most important characteristics of God in Islam are his oneness (*tawhid*), his transcendent otherness and his power. "*Allahu Akbar*," the traditional Muslim cry, means "God is great." It is a terrible blasphemy and unforgivable sin to associate anything with God; hence the vehement rejection of the Christian concept of the Trinity and of the phrase "Son of God."

There is much debate currently amongst Christians about the etymology of the word "Allah" and several theories are in circulation. It certainly existed in the Arabic language in pre-Islamic times, carrying the meaning of the supreme God, creator of the universe. But trying to track down the meaning a word had many centuries ago is not really very illuminating; after all the English word "God" is derived from a pagan term used in pre- Christian times, but rightly this does not trouble English-speaking Christians who give it their own meaning based on the Bible. Languages do evolve over time and words are "borrowed" from one context to be used in another. What is important today is to grasp what Muslims mean when they use the word "Allah." (See page 54.)

"Allah" is the word in both ancient and modern Arabic for "God." It is used by Arab Christians to mean their heavenly Father. It is found in the Arabic Bible wherever the word "God" is needed, for example, Genesis 1, John 1:1 and John 3:16. It was also used by Arab Christians in pre-Islamic times.

Eschatology

Muslims believe there will be catastrophic signs of the End Times which include the rise of the *dajjal* (antichrist) and the return of Jesus as a Muslim to defeat the *dajjal* and convert everyone to Islam. Most Muslims, and especially Shi'as, also believe in a coming End-Time messianic figure, the Mahdi, who will rule justly for a period. This will be followed by a general resurrection on the final Day of Judgment in which humans will be judged according to their deeds. The wicked (including all non-Muslims) will be assigned to hell, the just will enter paradise. Both paradise and hell are subdivided into various levels. Jesus is in only the second level of paradise, Moses is far above him in the sixth and Abraham in the seventh. Muhammad is in the highest level of paradise, just below God's throne. Some good Muslims – and especially those who die as martyrs for the cause of Islam – may go straight to paradise but many Muslims will have to spend time suffering in a purgatory-like stage before being allowed into paradise.

Angels and jinn

Angels are God's supernatural messengers created from light who watch over humans and record their good and bad deeds. The greatest angel is Gabriel (Jibrail) who is also called the Holy Spirit (*Ruh ul'Amin*). *Jinn* are spirits created by God from fire. Although some *jinn* are good, many of them are evil. Satan is sometimes described as a *jinn*, sometimes as an angel.

The five pillars

These five basic requirements of Islam mark Muslims as distinct from followers of other religions, signifying their submission, obedience, dependence and willingness to sacrifice.

1. Frequent recitation of the basic creedal declaration of faith (*shahada* or *kalmia*): "There is no god but God, and Muhammad is the apostle[10] of God." It is significant that Muhammad is included in this declaration – submission to God signifies submission to Muhammad's message and example.

2. Ritual prayers (*salat*) in the Arabic language at five appointed daily hours (dawn, noon, mid-afternoon, sunset and nightfall), accompanied by ceremonial washings and postures.

3. Fasting (*sawm*) from sunrise to sunset during the month of Ramadan. The fast includes abstinence from food, drink, sexual relations and smoking. Nowadays there is a huge celebratory feast every evening, as a result of which more food is consumed in Muslim countries during Ramadan than in a normal month.

4. The compulsory giving of alms (*zakat*) as a proportion of one's wealth (usually 2.5% for Sunnis). Some goes to help the poor and some to help those who fight in *jihad*.[11] Most Muslims hold that *zakat* cannot normally be given to non-Muslims. The definition given in the glossary of *The Noble Qur'an*, a widely distributed English translation of the Qur'an, states clearly that *zakat* is "for the benefit of the poor in the Muslim community."[12]

5. The pilgrimage to Mecca (*hajj*) is compulsory at least once in a lifetime for those in good health who can afford it. This includes wearing special clothes and engaging in specified rites, including circling seven times the *ka'ba* (the cube-like building at the centre of the Great Mosque).

Jihad

While not normally included in the five pillars (though some Muslims do add it as a sixth pillar), the struggle for Islam (*jihad*) is one of the most basic religious duties glorified in the Qur'an and *hadith* and prescribed in Islamic law (*shari'a*). "In all such cases, Jihad is as much a primary duty of the Muslims concerned as are the daily prayers or fasting."[13]

There are non-violent aspects of *jihad* such as financial sacrifice, the spiritual battle for moral purity, and using the tongue and hands to correct what is wrong and support what is right, but "in the language of Shari'ah this word is used particularly for a war that is waged solely in the name of Allah against those who practise oppression as enemies of Islam."[14]

The Noble Qur'an defines *jihad* in its glossary as follows:

Holy fighting in the Cause of Allah or any other kind of effort to make Allah's Word (i.e. Islam) superior. *Jihad* is regarded as one of the fundamentals of Islam.[15]

A footnote to sura 2, verse 190 (a key verse on *jihad*) states: "*Al-jihad* (holy fighting) in Allah's Cause (with full force of numbers and weaponry) is given the utmost importance in Islam and is one of its pillars (on which it stands)." It goes on to explain that *jihad* is the means by which Islam and its creed are established and propagated. According to this footnote, *jihad* is an obligatory duty for every Muslim and any who try to avoid it or even in their hearts do not wish to fulfil it "dies with one of the qualities of a hypocrite."[16] Those who raise armed *jihad* to the status of a "sixth pillar" make it a required duty for Muslims.

In early Islam *jihad* was seen as the God-given method for the expansion of Islam's political domain until all polytheists convert (or are killed) and Jews and Christians humbly submit themselves to Islamic domination. This understanding was consolidated in the teachings of classical Islam formulated over the next few centuries.[17]

Territory

Linked to the interpretation of *jihad* as the means of expanding Islam's political control is the classical Islamic concept of dividing the world into two domains: the House of Islam (*Dar al-Islam*) where political power is in the hands of Muslims and *shari'a* is enforced, and the House of War (*Dar al-Harb*). It is a religious duty for Muslims until the Day of Judgment to fight the House of War and transform it into the House of Islam.

Religious territoriality is an essential part of Islam, and Muslims are very conscious of whether or not they "control" any particular piece of land. They believe they must never yield any of their territory to non-Muslims, which is one of the reasons that many Muslims cannot conceive of any resolution to the Palestinian issue apart from the establishment of an Islamic state in place of Israel (a state in which Jews may or may not be permitted to live as a minority). The concept also has implications in the West, both in terms of town planning and in terms of how church leaders might choose to respond to requests by local Muslims for using church premises for their activities. Once a place has been used for Islamic worship, it is considered to "belong" to Islam for ever. (See also pages 75,83-84.)

Shari'a

Islamic law (*shari'a*) is based on Qur'an and *hadith*, and is an all-encompassing legalistic structure for the Islamic way of life, determining what is forbidden (*haram*) and what is permitted (*halal*). It contains detailed instructions for personal daily life and how to practice the pillars of Islam. The spectrum is subdivided into various degrees of obligatory, recommended, neutral, objectionable and forbidden. There is no individuality and no choice. In the eyes of most Muslims there is also no potential for any change to the *shari'a* regulations formulated in the eighth and ninth centuries AD.

Shari'a covers personal devotional life, family life, criminal law, the conduct of war, international relations and every aspect of life. *Shari'a* is given by God, the only sovereign legislator, for all times, and its implementation is an absolute command. It is also the only criterion of right and wrong:

> The Shari'ah itself is therefore the ultimate criterion of justice and mercy, and cannot and ought not to be measured against human standards.[18]

This statement becomes very relevant when it is considered how far the *shari'a* does deviate from modern standards of human rights and religious liberty. It is discriminatory against women and against non-Muslims. For example, the compensation payable to an individual after an injury is less for a woman and for a non-Muslim than for a Muslim man with the same injury. Likewise the value of their testimony in a law-court is less than that of a Muslim man. There is a whole raft of legislation in the *shari'a* to restrict the rights of non-Muslims. (See pages 72-74.)

Da'wa (Islamic mission)

Islam is a missionary religion and all Muslims have a duty to witness to their faith and win converts.

> The Qur'an clearly states that witnessing to the Truth in a manner that would leave mankind with no justifiable ground to deny it is the only purpose behind constituting you as a distinct Ummah (community), named Muslims ... this is no ordinary duty: it is a duty enjoined on you by Allah. It is a Divine command and a Divine call.[19]

Islamic *da'wa*, however, goes beyond gaining individual converts. It is seen as a communal responsibility aimed at extending the political and legal domain of Islam at the expense of all "unbelievers" (*kuffar*). It includes the strategy of keeping non-Muslim society – including the press and legislature – occupied with Islamic agendas, as part of the process of making society conform to Islam. The Muslim Brotherhood has developed an overall strategic plan to transform the character of North American society and establish the dominion of Islam.[20] *Da'wa* also includes the strategy of neutralizing all forms of Christian mission to Muslims, so that Muslims are protected from the Christian Gospel.

In recent decades a wide range of *da'wa* agencies has been created, using methods ranging from television right through to pamphlets, from apologetics to testimonies of converts. It is interesting to note that the majority of *da'wa* organizations in the US were started by Muslim professionals such as doctors, engineers, university lecturers etc. Because Islam does not separate religion from state, *da'wa* is also seen as part of the foreign policy of Muslim countries, many of which have also founded *da'wa* organizations which are something between a missionary society and a political party. Saudi Arabia, Iran and Libya are at the forefront of "missionary states." All these *da'wa* organizations have abundant funding from oil-rich Arab states and are able to be very active in community development in impoverished countries. They have studied all the successful methods used by Christian missionaries. Such commitment and such budgets pose a strong challenge to Christian mission today.

Islam replaces Christianity

Muslims hold that the Qur'an replaced the Old and New Testaments as God's written revelation valid today for all human beings. They claim that the text of the Bible has been corrupted by Jews and Christians, so is untrustworthy. At the same time Muhammad replaces Jesus as the Perfect Man, the God-given perfect example. The Qur'an even asserts that Jesus himself predicted the coming of Islam and Muhammad.[21]

While asserting that Muhammad is a normal human being with no supernatural powers who served simply as God's mouthpiece, Muslims have in practice elevated him into a Christ-like figure. (See page 19.) So, while paying lip service to their belief in Jewish and Christian scriptures and prophets, Muslims actually claim that Islam has superseded them and is the only valid religion for humanity today. It could be termed the ultimate "replacement theology."

Social issues

No separation of religion and state/society

Most Muslims consider the secular division of religion from the state as rebellion against God. They firmly believe in the unity of state and religion – Islam is both religion and state. Mosques, in contrast to churches, have always been centers of political agitation and intrigue. This view is the reason for the constant demands for state recognition of separate self-governing Muslim communities in the West. It also fuels the demands within Muslim-majority countries for the creation of true Islamic states governed by *shari'a*. In many Muslim countries, the state is intimately involved in religious affairs, often controlling the mosques and the clerical establishment as well as Islamic charitable foundations. Opposition to regimes is often expressed in Islamic terms, thus gaining respectability and popular support.

Individual and community

Central to a proper understanding of Islam is the realization that the community takes priority over the individual. Thus an individual's needs and choices must always be subjected to the good of the wider group in any case of conflict of interest. This wider group would be firstly the (extended) family, and secondly the entire Muslim nation worldwide, the *umma*.

The *umma* is a global community of faith, which is supposed to transcend race, nationality and culture. It is this that gives the Muslim his or her primary identity. This is not just a theoretical concept but is meant to have practical application in that when one Muslim is suffering or ill-treated the whole Muslim community should rally to his or her defense. The result is that Muslims tend to forget their differences and "close ranks" in the face of an outside threat. Muslims also show a passionate and unwavering loyalty to each other when it comes to advancing the cause of Islam or defending its honor.

The same principle of community taking priority over the individual is reflected in the coercive nature of the *shari'a*.

Loyalties

For many Muslims, loyalty to the global Muslim nation (the *umma*) overrides loyalty to any nation-state. In the orthodox view, politics is the means of advancing the cause of the whole worldwide Muslim community, of expanding Muslim control over as much territory as possible and governing it according to the *shari'a*. According to this view, Muslims in non-Muslim states have an overriding loyalty to further the cause of Islamizing their host-societies even when this undermines their loyalty to the state.

Because of the differences, disunity and fragmentation which exist in the Islamic world, there has arisen a desire to create unity by re-establishing the Islamic caliphate which came to an end in 1924 when Mustafa Kemal Atatürk abolished the Ottoman caliphate and proclaimed the Republic of Turkey.

The issue of loyalties is a point of contention within contemporary Islam, as the classical position described above comes into conflict with the concept of belonging to a nation-state, a concept to which some modern Muslims do subscribe but which many others believe is un-Islamic.

Spirituality,[22] morality and culture

Focus on the external

Islam is often seen primarily as a religion of externals, in which outward conformity to rituals and rules is often considered more important than the question of inner sincerity. It is thus a religion which lends itself to enforcement by the state. For example, some Muslims believe that the recitation of the creed, even without inner conviction, is sufficient to convert a person to Islam. Another example is the Muslim concept of fasting, which is very much a communal and visible act, which must be seen to be done. This is in complete contrast to Jesus' instructions on fasting in which he specifically told his followers to try not to let other people realize that they were fasting (Matthew 6:16-18). Christian fasting is a private act of self-denial between the individual and God. Muslim fasting is a public act which, hard though it may be through the hours of daylight, involves a daily banquet of vast quantities of delicacies.

The whole issue of the relationship of faith to Islam and of the term "Muslim" to the term "believer" as well as the need or otherwise for inner belief has historically been a subject of much debate within Islam. The Sufi movement within Islam (see pages 45-46) emphasizes the inner life and personal devotion to God. Muslims may also seek an inner spiritual experience through Muhammad veneration (widely practiced on the Indian subcontinent) and various non-orthodox practices such as the ecstatic ceremonies of the whirling dervishes, the self-injury of many Shi'a sects and visiting the shrines of Muslim saints.

Given the emphasis on externals, it is perhaps little surprise that Islam primarily concentrates on material blessings rather than, say, the delights of fellowship with God. Paradise is full of sensual pleasures in which there are beautiful women, couches covered with brocades, plentiful wine and luscious fruits. Essentially it is the place where that which is forbidden on earth becomes allowed. There are today some Muslims who are seeking to interpret these heavenly promises in spiritual terms. They look forward to seeing at last in paradise the "unseeable" Allah, even if only for a moment. But historically the understanding has been literal and physical and still is for many Muslims today.

Fear and lack of assurance of salvation

The Muslim's submission to God is born out of a fear of his sovereignty and overwhelming power. There are a variety of beliefs among Muslims about getting to paradise, but the bottom line is that God is remote and does as he wills in all things, so the outcome of God's judgment is unpredictable: he will save or condemn as he pleases and will not necessarily take into account the individual's conduct while on earth. Therefore, in spite of obedience to *shari'a*, living a pious life and performing good works, few can be sure of their eternal destiny. Even those who believe that all Muslims will eventually get to paradise hold that some may have to undergo a period of frightful punishment first. But one sure way to go straight to paradise – avoiding any punishment on the way – is to die as a martyr in *jihad*.

Freedom of conscience

Muslims have no freedom or choice in matters of religion. Islam is a one-way street which once entered cannot be forsaken. Leaving Islam is seen as treachery against God and against society, and therefore the penalty is death, as laid down in the *shari'a*. In addition there are a host of other legal penalties for apostates from Islam.

A few modern states have implemented the death penalty, but even where this is not enshrined in the law of the land, or not enforced, converts from Islam may find themselves punished by the authorities on some other pretext or intimidated and victimized by family and community who feel shamed by the "traitor". Many are physically attacked and some are even murdered.

Vulnerability and superiority

Richard Chartres, the Anglican Bishop of London, has said, "There is an immense sense in Islam of the superiority of Islam to everything else."[23] Believing that it is the final and ultimate religion, Islam finds it difficult to affirm other faiths. One symptom of this is the fact that all of history prior to Muhammad is termed "the age of ignorance" implying that nothing good can be learnt from it. Neither can anything good be learnt from later non-Islamic contexts. Muslims will very rarely accept blame for evils committed in the name of Islam, or apologize to their victims. The shame of losing face would keep many from even contemplating such an admission.

Muslims usually interpret confession of guilt by others as a sign of despicable weakness. Likewise, humility and forgiveness are not seen as virtues but as weaknesses. They hold that the appropriate reaction to being wronged is to seek revenge. Muslims have very long historical memories and continue to remember with outrage the defeats and humiliations of many centuries ago even if they were suffered by far distant parts of the *umma*. What Charles Moore has termed "pre-emptive self-abasement"[24] – the Western (and perhaps especially British) penchant for offering profuse apologies for all faults, past or present, real or imagined – is at best useless, but more likely to be counter-productive. This is important for Christians to remember when engaged in "dialogue" or debate with Muslims.

Power and honor

An important part of Islamic self-understanding is the concept that power and honor rightly belong to Muslims. The basis of this is found in the Qur'an (sura 63, verse 8)

... But honour, power and glory belong to Allah and to His
Messenger (Muhammad), and to the believers"[25]

The Arabic word translated here as "honor, power and glory"
appears in some other translations simply as "honor". The longer
translation correctly conveys the connotations of dominion and
control which Muslims understand when they read this text. For
Muslims temporal power, the advance of the Islamic faith, military
victory and the prestige of Muslim people are all intrinsically linked
to this promise. Humiliation and defeat are against God's plan for his
people and when these occur they cause grave anguish to Muslims as
they have no theology to deal with such situations.

> By abandoning Jihad (may Allah protect us from that) Islam is
> destroyed and the Muslims fall into an inferior position; their honour
> is lost, their lands are stolen, their rule and authority vanish.[26]

As Bishop Richard Chartres has said, Islam's sense of its own
superiority

> is in terrible full-frontal collision with the evident inferiority of
> Muslim societies, technically, politically, economically, militarily.
> And the crisis in Islam (it's not so much a battle between East and
> West, Christians and Muslims, it's a battle in Islam) comes from
> the terrible collision of this sense of superiority with the evident
> inferiority in so many other ways which causes bewilderment
> and fierce debate on how we are going to get out of this bind.[27]

There is no real critical assessment within Islam of its own history
and thus the glorification of early Islam and its expansion is seen as
a Golden Age of Islam, which needs to be recreated in order finally
to conquer the whole world for Islam.

Shame and guilt

Contrary to Christianity, it is shame rather than guilt which is the
guiding principle in Islam. Shame is most easily defined by looking at

its opposite, honor. Honor includes self-esteem and dignity, and the good opinion of others. It depends very much on the reputation of an individual and his family for generosity, morality, good behavior, courage, good marriages, piety and loyalty to kin. The individual is expected to suppress his or her personal needs and interests if they interfere with family or community honor.

Public loss of face is the greatest possible shame, so blunt criticism (seen as a personal insult) must be avoided and praise must preface any indirect criticism, which must never be given in front of others.

Honor is more important than truth and even than life itself. Honor, of which a large part is the appearance of morality and the reputation for morality, is more important than morality itself. The deep fear of the loss of honor explains why some will kill people they love rather than be disgraced. If an incident causing loss of honor is not avenged, a man becomes permanently dishonored and shamed. Sullied honor demands payment to restore the balance – payment ruled by traditional rituals of mediation and reconciliation. Ignoring these rituals leaves the offender open to violent revenge not only against himself but also against his family.

Women and family honor

A family's honor is especially bound up in the behavior of its women who must be seen to dress and behave modestly. Maintaining proper relationships between the sexes is the responsibility of a man of honor who must control the women in his family so that they do nothing unseemly. Any hint of a sexual misdemeanor is considered a crime against family honor and must be punished to restore the depleted honor account.

Honor killings

The phrase "honor killings" generally refers to the practice of killing female family members who have behaved in an improper way. So strong is the drive to restore family honor that many women and girls have been killed for apparently minor offences, such as speaking to an unrelated man. They are often killed on the basis of a mere accusation, without proof of their crime. In societies where the concept of honor killing is very strong, for example Pakistan, the law enforcement agencies will do little or nothing to punish the murderer. It has recently become clear that many honor killings occur also within the Muslim communities of Western Europe.

The Muslim family

Muslim families tend to be conservative and patriarchal; the oldest male is usually recognized as head of the extended family, and fathers are the source of authority and discipline. The relationship between husband and wife is not expected to be close and fond; it is more a practical arrangement – one is the provider of money, the other the provider of sons. A man may have up to four wives if he treats them all equally. The closest family bond is often between a mother and her sons.

The extended family determines an individual's identity, position and status in society and to a large extent the chance of success and wealth. People are proud of their family connections and lineage. Loyalty to the family takes precedence over personal needs, obligations to friends or the demands of a job. A person's first allegiance will always be to their relatives, and a basic rule is that no one can really be trusted except family members. The family is the main source of emotional and economic security, and relatives are expected to help each other, including financial help when necessary.

The family is the most important factor in all decisions, including matters of religion, marriage and jobs. All social institutions are imagined as family: rulers see their citizens as their children and themselves as fathers of the nation. The same applies to teachers, employers, and political and religious leaders.

Women

In pre-Islamic Arabia women of the elite strata of society could be active participants, even leaders, in a wide range of community activities including warfare and religion. On the other hand poorer women were regarded as mere chattels of men, and female infanticide was practiced. Such freedoms as the women had were curtailed when Islam was established, for its institution of patrilineal patriarchal marriage brought a social transformation. Muslims often claim that Muhammad improved the situation of women, but they usually fail to add that Islam also fixed their status for ever at a seventh century level.

The position accorded to women in the *shari'a* is certainly not one of equality with men. The various regulations concerned with women indicate an underlying, if unspoken, assumption that women are inferior to men in intelligence, morals and religion. They are therefore considered a source of temptation to men, and must be protected from their own weaknesses. This is tied up with the concept that a family's honor resides in its womenfolk. The primary requirement of a woman is obedience to her husband (rather than to God directly). Some Islamic scholars argue that most women will go to hell.

Because of this aspect of Islam, it is rare for Muslim women and girls to be as well taught in their religion as the men and boys are. Most women therefore tend to follow folk Islam and may be very ignorant of the teachings of true Islam. Ironically, it is the women who watch over the faith of the family and ensure that the traditions of Islam are transmitted to the next generation, while the men are more prominent in public affairs.

Taqiyya (dissimulation, permitted deceit)

It often comes as a surprise to realize that protective deceit and dissimulation are an intrinsic part of Islam, permitted in certain specific situations, one of which is war, i.e. the defense of Islam. Some Muslims also hold that it is permissible to break agreements made with non- Muslims, believing such contracts to be valid only as long as they serve the cause of Islam. It is important for non- Muslims interacting with Muslims to be aware of the existence of *taqiyya*, as the concept of "defending Islam" can be interpreted very broadly and may lead to outright lying. What is said in English to Christians one day might be totally contradicted the next day by the same leaders speaking to Muslims, perhaps in Urdu or Arabic. For example, Hamid Ali, spiritual leader of Al-Madina Masjid, a mosque in Beeston, West Yorkshire, UK publicly condemned the London bombings of July 7, 2005. But in a secretly taped conversation with a Bangladeshi-origin undercover reporter from *The Sunday Times* he said the 7/7 bombings were a "good" act and praised the bombers as "children" of firebrand cleric Abdullah al-Faisal who has made statements such as: "The only way forward is for you, the Muslims, to kill the *kufrs* (non-believers)." [28]

As Dr Taj Hargey, Chairman of the Muslim Education Centre, Oxford, explained on British television:

> We have one vocabulary in private and we have another vocabulary
> for the public domain and that's why you don't hear it because
> you're the public domain.[29]

Islam nominally places a high value on truth and one of the 99 names of God is *al-Haqq* (the Reality, the Supreme Truth). Alongside this runs the doctrine of *taqiyya* which was first developed for dealing with situations of persecution where Muslims could save their lives by concealing their true beliefs. The Qur'anic basis is sura 16, verse 106, which absolves Muslims from God's wrath if they are forced into outward disbelief while in their hearts they remain true Muslims.

Whoever disbelieved in Allah after his belief, except him who is forced thereto and whose heart is at rest with Faith; but such as open their breasts to unbelief, on them is wrath from Allah, and theirs will be a great torment.

Various *hadith* provide more details of when lying is permissible, typically in three situations: to one's wife, in war, and for the purpose of reconciliation. *Taqiyya* is particularly strong amongst Shi'a Muslims but also practiced by Sunnis.

At a Palestine Solidarity Movement conference held at Georgetown University, Washington DC (February 17-19, 2006) two workshops looked at how the participants could win Christians to their cause (the elimination of Israel). Participants were told to "target" small churches, and win the trust of church members by "looking and acting Christian." They were told to wear Western-style clothes, be well-groomed and speak nicely. "If someone sneezes, say God bless you. And always come bearing gifts, especially something from the Holy Land like holy water or rosary beads." They were advised to get involved with the church community. "Don't look down on the church ladies' clubs – join them."[30] This deliberate deception is part of *taqiyya*.

One of the ways in which *taqiyya* is manifested in the West today is the rewriting of history and in the mantra-like repetitive assertion that "Islam is peace." The Muslim version of history, as presented all too often in school textbooks as well as TV programs and exhibitions, manages on the one hand to exclude all the negative aspects of Islam such as conquest, slavery and empire, and on the other hand to present Islam as being followed at ludicrously unlikely times and places. Thus Westerners are told that Islam arrived in Australia in the ninth century AD[31] and in North America before Christopher Columbus got there.[32] They are told that Napoleon Bonaparte was a Muslim, as was Offa the eighth century Saxon King of Mercia. It is even suggested that William Shakespeare followed a kind of Islamic mysticism.

Likewise the historical achievements of Islam in the arts and sciences are exaggerated, while the oppression of non-Muslim minorities and of women is minimized. The take-home message is that European civilization is based on Islamic civilization. The fact that Islamic civilization itself drew heavily on the learning of Greek, Hindu and other cultures is underplayed, as is the fact that many of the individuals within the Muslim world who contributed most to the achievements of "Islamic" civilization were actually *dhimmi*, i.e. the Jews and Christians living in the midst of the Muslims.

Islamic theology is often presented in the West in a way which conceals its faults and magnifies its virtues. This can be part of *da'wa* or simply a prudent tactic for creating a favorable image of the Muslim minority to the majority society. Non-Muslims tend to be vulnerable to this kind of propaganda because of their lack of knowledge about Islam. Four fallacies about the Islamic faith which are frequently heard in the West are as follows:

- *The word "Islam" means "peace".* In fact, it means "submission". (See page 18.)
- *Islam is a religion of peace and there are many verses to prove this in the Qur'an.* There are indeed many peaceable verses in the Qur'an but they are abrogated (canceled) by later-dated warlike verses. (See page 53.) Furthermore, it is essential to remember that the Qur'an is not the only source of Islamic law. The *hadith* are also very important, and they record many warlike words and examples. So the important question to ask is not "What does the Qur'an say?" but "What does the *shari'a* say?" This is very different from the situation in Christianity where the Bible alone is the ultimate source of doctrine. So arguments based solely on the content of the Qur'an can be

misleading; it all depends how the Qur'an is interpreted in classical Orthodox Islam.

- *The Qur'an says: "If you kill one soul it is as if you killed all mankind."* These or similar words, often quoted to prove that Islam is only peaceable, are a misquote. The actual Qur'anic text runs: "If anyone killed a person not in retaliation of murder, or (and) to spread mischief in the land – it would be as if he killed all mankind" (sura 5, verse 32). The very next verse lists a selection of savage punishments for those who wage war against God and Muhammad and make "mischief" (or in some translations "corruption") in the land. These punishments include execution, crucifixion and amputation. The meaning of the verse depends on what is understood by "retaliation of murder" and "mischief in the land" i.e. on what justifies killing. Some Muslims interpret "mischief in the land" as meaning secularism, democracy and other non-Islamic values in a land. Some consider that "murder" includes the killing of Muslims in Iraq by American or British forces. Some go so far as to view the "war on terror" as a Judeo-Christian scheme to destroy Islam.

- *The Qur'an says: "There is no compulsion in religion," which proves that there is full religious liberty in Islam.* The quote is accurate (from sura 2, verse 256) but the interpretation is a special one for Westerners. The normal Muslim interpretation of this verse is that Muslims will not be forced to fulfill all their religious duties, it is up to them whether they do so or not. This verse has nothing to say about freedom of conscience, which is severely restricted in Islam, given that Muslims are not permitted to leave their faith. In any case, it is an early verse, so many consider it to have been abrogated by later verses.

Curses

Sometimes cursing prayers against Christians (and – even more so – against Jews) are used at Friday prayers in the mosque. The practice of cursing Christians, Jews and infidels in general (i.e. non-Muslims) is based on verses in the Qur'an.

> Verily, those who conceal the clear proofs, evidences and the guidance, which We have sent down, after We have made it clear for the people in the Book, they are the ones cursed by Allah and cursed by the cursers.[33]

> And the Jews say: 'Uzair (Ezra) is the son of Allah, and the Christians say: Messiah is the son of Allah. That is their saying with their mouths, resembling the saying of those who disbelieved aforetime. Allah's Curse be upon them, how they are deluded away from the truth![34]

It is also based on examples in the *hadith* such as:.

> ... Allah's Apostle further said, "May Allah curse the Jews, for Allah made the fat (of animals) illegal for them, yet they melted the fat and sold it and ate its price.[35]

> On his death-bed Allah's Apostle put a sheet over his face and when he felt hot, he would remove it from his face. When in that state (of putting and removing the sheet) he said, "May Allah's Curse be on the Jews and the Christians for they build places of worship at the graves of their prophets."...[36]

Some Muslims are uncomfortable with the idea of cursing non-Muslims indiscriminately. A *fatwa* issued by "a group of *muftis*" on October 30, 2003 addressed this concern and said that it was only permissible to curse non-Muslims who were at war with Muslims or seeking to harm them. A *fatwa* from a scholar at Al-Azhar University, Cairo, the leading centre of Sunni Islam, said that such prayers were part of *jihad* and resisting oppression or injustice.[37]

An article in the March 10, 2008 edition of the Saudi pro-government daily newspaper *Al-Jazirah* nonetheless described how "in almost every sermon, without exception imams recite supplications against Jews and Christians, and ask God [Allah] that we defeat them, capture their women, and confiscate their possessions as booty."[38] This supplication, the writer Fahd al-Hushani said, "calls for the destruction of whole states even if they have Muslims living in them."

Some examples of cursing prayers are as follows:

> O Allah, destroy the *kuffar* (infidels i.e. non-Muslims) who are trying to prevent people from following Your path, who deny Your Messengers and who do not believe in Your promise (the Day of Judgment). Make them disunited, fill their hearts with terror and send Your wrath and punishment against them, O God of Truth.[39]

> O God, destroy the Jews and their supporters and the Christians and their supporters and followers. O God, destroy the ground under their feet, instil fear in their hearts, and freeze the blood in their veins. (From the Grand Mosque in Sanaa, Yemen)

> O God, destroy the Jews and their supporters, including the crusaders and some so-called Muslims. O God, use your power against them. (From the Umar Bin-al-Khattab Mosque in Doha, Qatar)

> O God, destroy the Jews and Americans for they are within your power. O God, show them a black day. O God, shake the ground under their feet, weaken them, hang their flags at half mast, down their planes, and drown their ships. (From the Abu-Hanifah al-Nu'man mosque in Baghdad, Iraq)

O Allah, perish America, Christians and their allies. O God, destroy their homes, widow their women and make their children orphans! O God, destroy all the Jews and Christians. (From a mosque in an Arab country) [40]

Night prayer during Ramadan appears to be a time when cursing prayers are quite often used.[41] Christians who do a special month of prayer for Muslims during Ramadan should be aware of this spiritual dimension. At the very least they should be sure to pray for protection for themselves, for unity amongst Christians and for a strong faith, remembering that death, destruction, disunity and fear are the main things which the cursing prayers ask for.

Curses are often included in the *qunoot* prayers offered after regular morning prayers in mosques whenever the *umma* seems to be experiencing trouble, for example natural disaster, plague or war. One pattern for such a prayer is:

O Allah, let Your curse be on those unbelievers who prevent people from treading Your path, who reject Your prophets and fight Your chosen ones. O Allah, make difficult their plans, shake their feet and give them such punishment which is not turned away from a sinning people.[42]

Diversity in Islam

The complexity of Islam, and the diversity of opinion within it, cannot be over-emphasized.

Major divisions

Following Muhammad's death in 632, he was succeeded in sequence by four of his most trusted companions – Abu Bakr, Umar, Uthman and Ali, the "Rightly Guided Caliphs." The three major groupings within Islam arose from disagreements about the line of succession.

Sunnis

The Sunnis held that any suitable person from Muhammad's tribe, the Quraysh, was eligible to be elected as caliph. Sunni empires and states have dominated the Muslim world throughout its history and Sunnis comprise the great majority of Muslims today (at least 80%).

In the last two centuries Sunni Islam has become increasingly dominated by Wahhabism, a puritanical movement which originated in the Arabian peninsula. Wahhabism is being promoted worldwide with Saudi money. Wahhabis reject all cultural manifestations such as folk Islam. They reject the standard schools of *shari'a* and later developments in Islam and demand a return to the early model of Muhammad and his Companions and their followers, the first three generations in Islam. They limit religious authority to the Qur'an and *hadith* interpreted in a literalist manner.

Shi'as

The Shi'as, who today comprise something under 20% of all Muslims, believe that only Ali, Muhammad's cousin and son-in-law, and Ali's male descendants are the legitimate successors to Muhammad. Their hopes were frustrated when Ali's reign ended with his assassination and his son Hussein was killed whilst seeking to regain the caliphate.

Shi'a Islam touches the emotions much more than does Sunni Islam; self-denial and martyrdom are strongly emphasized.

The Shi'as are today a majority in Iran, Iraq, Azerbaijan and Bahrain. There are significant Shi'a minorities in Yemen, Lebanon, some other Gulf states and the Indian subcontinent. Shi'a Islam has split into numerous sects including the Isma'ilis (who once established the magnificent Fatimid Empire in Egypt, but are now a scattered minority, led mainly by the Agha Khan). In Turkey there is a significant Shi'a minority, the Alevis, who revere Ali as an incarnation of God.

Kharijis

The third group of early Muslims, the Kharijis, rejected both Sunni and Shi'a claims, arguing that the position of caliph should be open to any suitable Muslim, no matter what their tribe or family. The Kharijis were a constant source of rebellion and civil war against mainstream Islam for several centuries. They were finally crushed and virtually exterminated so that only tiny remnants, now peaceful, survive today in Oman and North Africa, where they are called respectively Ibadis and Mzabis.

Sufism[43]

There are many individual Muslims, both Sunni and Shi'a, who hunger for an inner spiritual reality. They may seek this in Sufism, that is, Islamic mysticism, which is very much concerned with the sincerity of intention. A main goal of Sufism is mystical union with God. It also stresses the intercessory power of Muslim saints.

Amongst Sufism's distinctives are the importance of knowledge of God's commands and remembrance (*dhikr* or *zikr*) of him by devotional chanting etc. The goal of *dhikr* is purification of the heart, producing in it the love of God and a consciousness of his greatness as well as peace, fulfillment and contentment. Sufism focuses on the hereafter and on seeking divine approval, rather than on material blessing in the present world. It emphasizes both an inner discipline and also conformity to the Islamic code of social conduct. Sufism can also involve the concept of the "warrior saint" and Sufis have been active in rebellion and militant dissent, for example, against their colonial masters. It is not, as sometimes thought, a "pacifist branch of Islam."

Sufism is rejected by Wahhabis as not truly Islamic; they consider it theologically suspect and some of its doctrines even blasphemous. It is, however, a type of Islam which appeals particularly to white Westerners, with some converting to Sufism.

Folk Islam

Islam is not just built on theological premises and the five pillars but also undergirded by culture. The cultural aspects include pre-Islamic Arabian culture as well as accretions of the cultures of the various other peoples who became Muslim as Islam expanded.[44] Together with Qur'anic and *hadith* passages about evil spiritual powers (especially *jinn*) and aspects of Sufism, these constitute "folk Islam." It is widespread among the poor and uneducated, but impacts all levels of Muslim society, running in parallel with orthodox Islam.

Folk Islam is primarily concerned with using spiritual powers to meet felt needs such as healing of illness, exorcism and protection from evil *jinn*. Much time and energy are devoted to trying to influence spiritual powers in one's favor, using amulets, vows, curses, invocations of God's name, and the placing of Qur'anic verses around the home or person, etc. God is considered far away and unknowable, but Muslim saints are seen as accessible protectors from evil, intercessors with God, and sources of supernatural power. Their tombs and shrines are places of pilgrimage and prayer. A very important aspect of folk Islam is the veneration of Muhammad, who is considered a powerful intercessor.[45]

Other factors

As well as the theology of the caliphate succession there are other factors that divide the Muslim world. Ethnicity is one such factor, as seen in the Middle East where Sunni Kurds have fought against Sunni Turks and Arabs for decades, or in Nigeria where an ethnic Yoruba Muslim may even feel more loyalty to a Yoruba Christian than to an ethnic Hausa Muslim.

In other parts of the Islamic world, where social structures are largely feudal in nature such as Pakistan, Yemen or Oman, society may be divided into caste-like stratifications. In many societies in

Africa and Asia, Muslim and non-Muslim alike are divided by tribe, clan and kin group. However, the ideal is considered to be Arabic Islam because the final revelation was given to Muhammad, an Arab, and is recorded in heaven in Arabic.

Trends in contemporary Islam

Another analysis divides Muslims into three very broad categories representing different contemporary trends.

Conservatives

The overwhelming majority of the world's Muslims fall into this category. They are traditional and broadly orthodox in their beliefs, but also may be fairly nominal in their practice, doing little beyond fasting in Ramadan and praying when they can. Like most people of any religion, everyday realities such as raising families and finding work are of more immediate concern than the demands of their faith. Many will know little of Islam beyond the broad outlines, but these they would hold to with a strong conviction. (A comparison could be made with Europe in the Middle Ages, where virtually everyone firmly believed in Christianity, but for most it was not the defining focus or concern of their daily lives.) However, when confronted by a situation which throws their faith into stark relief most Muslims in this category would clearly identify themselves with a conservative Islamic position. Thus they would not engage in violence themselves but might well sympathize with and even finance Osama bin Laden and other militants whom they see as championing the Muslim world against its Western oppressors.

Broadly speaking this group is undergoing change in the direction of becoming more observant and more devout, a change which is manifested both in Muslim-majority contexts and in Muslim-minority contexts. Furthermore it is gradually losing members to both ends of the spectrum, that is, to the radicals (Islamists) and, to a lesser extent, the liberals.

Islamists

These are radically active Muslims who are dedicated to transforming society to conform with *shari'a*. They adhere to a very rigid and austere form of Islam and apply literally all aspects of classical Islamic teaching including the expansion of *Dar al-Islam* through military struggle. This category is much smaller than the conservatives but is growing due to the increasing radicalization of conservatives.

Islamists have a political agenda in their own home countries as well as in the West, with long-term strategies for the Islamization of the world. Some Islamists are willing to use "democratic methods" in the process of turning democracies into Islamic states. Other Islamists would be willing to engage in terror as a means to intimidate and conquer.

Liberals

Very much a minority and far smaller in number than the radicals, Muslims in this category have adapted their faith to conform to modernity. They are usually well educated and often live or have lived in the West. They accept without qualification the Western understanding of concepts such as human rights, democracy, equality and freedom of thought and speech, separation of state from religion, and are willing to engage in criticism of their own faith, culture and communities in support of these concepts. If Islamists can be said to believe that the modern world should adapt to Islam, modernists can be said to believe that Islam should adapt to the modern world. Some of these liberal intellectuals have been subject to huge pressure and threats from other Muslims to try to make them change their position. (See page 68-69 for some examples.)

Most liberals are not particularly devout, indeed many are so secularized that they have only a vestigial faith and could more properly be described as agnostic. Increasingly they have "privatized" their faith and cut themselves off from the formal practices of classical Islam as well as from Islam's past. Some have even rejected Islam altogether and embraced beliefs like atheism while remaining culturally Muslim.

There are also Muslims who are liberal in their outlook but conservative in their theology. Muslims of this kind had some influence on the wider Muslim community during the colonial and early post-colonial periods. (A prominent example would be Muhammad Ali Jinnah, the founder of Pakistan.) More recently however, with the growing influence of Islamists, their influence has waned. This position might be classified as "moderate," although that is a very confusing term used to cover a wide range of different stances. The important question with Muslim liberals is always how far they embrace Western secular values, especially the separation of state and religion, the value of the individual, freedom of choice and freedom of conscience.

Understanding what is happening in the Muslim world today

The European colonial period had a numbing effect on Islamic culture and thought. The once glorious civilizations of the Islamic world had so clearly been conquered and surpassed by Christian Europe in so many areas, and this prompted a degree of reflection and the adoption of Western ideals and concepts. Thus in the immediate post-colonial years the states that emerged in the Islamic world were almost all Western-style nation- states with Western-based constitutions and legislation.

However since the 1970s this has begun to change with increasing rapidity. Many Muslim leaders, reformers and intellectuals are feeling that borrowed ideals like nationalism, socialism, communism and capitalism have failed the Muslim world. They are increasingly rejecting the West, returning to traditional and literal applications of Islamic teaching, and looking for answers within their own historical and religious tradition. Various catalysts such as the huge financial investment by Saudi Arabia and other oil-rich Gulf states in promoting Islam, the Iranian revolution of 1979, the *jihad* in Afghanistan during the 1980s and more recently the wars of the early years of the twenty-first century in Afghanistan and Iraq have accelerated this process. A revival and resurgence is taking place within Islam today which will have enormous influence on the future of the whole world.

Comparing Islam with Christianity

Although Islam and Christianity have certain points of doctrine in common, such as a belief in one God, revealed scriptures and the Day of Judgment, there is an enormous difference between them in the crucial areas of understanding of God's nature, Christ and salvation, as well as in many other areas affecting daily lives, attitudes and worldviews. While they share some beliefs, on the most important ones their understandings are completely different.

Dr. R. Albert Mohler, Jr., president of the Southern Baptist Theological Seminary, stresses this in his writings for the *Newsweek/Washington Post* website, "On Faith," where he is a panelist.

> We may find common ground on some issues, but the Muslim worldview and the Christian worldview differ radically. No informed person should be unaware of the basic incompatibility of Christianity and Islam.[46]

If Christians plan to work together with Muslims, it is important that they recognize the deep theological differences between the two faiths, rather than pretend they are not important or claim they do not even exist. They must be aware that Islam challenges the core beliefs of the Church. An extra challenge is posed by the fact that Muslims use some of the same terminology as Christians do but with different meanings. So Christians must be aware that words like "God", "faith", "heaven", "holy scriptures", "grace" do not mean the same in Islam as in Christianity.

The real difference between Christianity and Islam lies in the issues of their sacred writings and the persons of their founders. Christians have frequently in their long history departed from Christ's teachings and perpetrated cruelties against Jews, Muslims and heretics. However, when returning to their source scriptures they come face to face with the person of Christ and the Gospel of love and forgiveness he preached, as well as his atoning death and supreme example of humility, service, suffering and non-violence.

When Muslims return to their original sources, they have a very different encounter. The later dated verses of the Qur'an, revealed to Muhammad in Medina, contain much that is intolerant and belligerent. According to the most commonly followed doctrine of abrogation, whenever the Qur'an is self-contradictory, later dated verses abrogate (cancel) earlier verses. So the Medina verses cancel the more peaceable verses dating from Muhammad's days in Mecca. Muslims also meet Muhammad whose words and actions, recorded in the *hadith*, give many clear examples of aggression, warmongering, even what in modern terminology appear to be assassination, torture and genocide. Some Muslims will argue that these actions were for a particular context only, but the fact remains that they occurred. Setting up Muhammad as the supreme example in every aspect of his words and actions, necessitates transforming his vices into virtues. This is the real cause of the contradictions so prevalent in Islamic societies and Islamic history, especially on issues relating to *jihad*, the treatment of women, and the contempt shown to non-Muslims.

Having made this comparison, it should be added that another vital difference is the relative importance of the founder and of the scriptures. The Christian faith is ultimately a relationship with a Person, but Islam is focused on the authority of a book.

God, the Trinitarian loving Father

The important question is not whether Muslims and Christians believe in "the same God," but what they understand his character to be. Christians understand the nature of God by looking into the face of Christ who revealed God to humanity. They believe God's primary attribute is love and call him Father. Christians also believe in a God who responds to humans' repentance and faith.

While Christians believe that God is both transcendent and immanent, Islam very much stresses God's transcendence. He is so "other" that he cannot be adequately described in human language, neither can he enter into the experiences of humanity, so he cannot suffer. An individual's relation to God is best described as slave to master. The Islamic teachings on predestination encourage passivity and fatalism, as no one can change what God has ordained.

Christians believe that Jesus is God's Son not in the carnal sense, but in the sense that he has the Father's eternal nature and attributes. The Trinity, although a divine mystery, is clearly attested in scripture and is the basis for our personal relationship with God. Muslims deny the Trinity, which they understand in terms of God having sexual relations with Mary who then bore Jesus. They state that God can have no son, and they view the Trinity as blasphemy, a pagan belief in three gods.

Jesus Christ

Christians view Christ as the second person of the Godhead, the Lord who is to be worshipped and adored. Christ's incarnation and substitutionary death on the cross are God's redemptive plan from all eternity, forming the basis of God's offer of free salvation to all who believe.

Muslims often claim to honor Jesus, yet they mean only that they consider him a prophet. They emphatically reject his deity[47] and

Sonship,[48] holding him to be a mere man. There is reference to this in the first half of the Islamic creed which states: "There is no god but God..." Although Islam reveres Jesus as a sinless[49] prophet[50] and miracle-worker,[51] it will be remembered that his place in heaven is only the second of seven levels. Islam accepts the virgin birth[52] and Christ's second coming (albeit as a Muslim),[53] but it denies Christ's crucifixion[54] and therefore his atoning sacrifice, and resurrection, claiming that someone else was crucified in his place. Islam thus denies the very heart and cornerstone of the Christian faith. Jesus is neither Lord nor Savior in Islam.

Christians believe that Christ is God's final revelation to mankind but Muslims believe that a later and final revelation was added when the message of the Qur'an was given to Muhammad. This is the thought behind the second half of the Islamic creed: "... and Muhammad is his messenger." The Islamic creed is in fact aimed at denying Christianity, especially the finality of Christ, and asserting the supremacy of Islam.

Mankind and the fall

Christians believe in mankind's inherent sinfulness which makes humans unable to redeem themselves. They are cast on God's mercy and grace in Christ. Through the work of the Holy Spirit lives and characters are transformed, which in turn affects community and society. Muslims deny the sinfulness of mankind due to the fall, viewing human nature as inherently good, though weak. There is thus no original sin and no necessity for God's intervention in redemption. Most Muslims have a utopian view of the perfectibility of man given the right environment (i.e. under *shari'a*), making checks and balances in politics and society unnecessary.

Christians see all humans as equal in worth because all are created in God's image (*imago dei*). Non-Christians are to be served in love and offered the Gospel freely. They are to be treated as equals and are not to suffer any disabilities because of their religion, race or gender.

Islam finds very offensive the view that humans are created in God's image. Muslims therefore do not consider that there is an innate equality of all people, the basis of human rights. Instead, Islam sets up a rigid social order, defined in the *shari'a*, which differentiates between Muslim and non-Muslim, and between male and female. Each category is treated differently: non-Muslims are of less value than Muslims and women of less value than men. Obligatory duties are emphasized rather than inherent rights.

Salvation and grace

For Christians, salvation means forgiveness of sins, acceptance into God's family, and the certainty of eternal life in heaven in God's presence. Christians believe salvation is an undeserved free gift of God's grace offered on the basis of Christ's atoning death.

Islam, however, offers a complete alternative to the Christian understanding of God's plan for redemption through Christ. In Islam salvation is through good works and religious rituals and there is no need for God's intervention in grace and atonement. On the Day of Judgment all one's good and bad deeds will be weighed in the divine scales. Muslims have no assurance of salvation as no one can predict whether their good deeds will outweigh their sins, or indeed what God may choose to do in his omnipotence. Paradoxically, because God does as he wills, the outcome of God's judgment is unpredictable: he will save or condemn whom he will regardless of their conduct. No one can be sure of their eternal destiny, except martyrs.

Mission

Christianity is a missionary religion with a mandate to preach the Gospel to all the world. However, it stresses the free choice of individuals in their response to the Gospel. The emphasis is on the individual's – not the community's – choice to love God and to follow Christ.

Christian mission should involve neither coercion nor deception. All should be done with openness, integrity and transparency. Christ calls us to be as wise as serpents but as gentle as doves. Christian mission should be done with vulnerability and the giving of oneself, a spirit that is free from arrogance and pride, being constrained by the love of Jesus. This is not to deny the sad fact that Christians have not always lived up to this teaching and that at times the Church has enforced conversions and severely punished heresy and apostasy. Similarly missionaries have sometimes used methods that have amounted to deceit in their eagerness to win converts.

Islam is also a missionary religion and all Muslims have the obligation to witness to their faith, win converts and Islamize other communities. This is an obligation which Muslims take seriously, so that ordinary devout Muslims are likely to be active in this area. Muslims use many methods for this *da'wa*, including efforts at the gradual Islamization of non-Muslim societal structures.

While freedom exists to propagate Islam in the West, most Muslim states severely restrict Christian mission or completely forbid it. Indeed Christian mission is one of the three greatest grievances which Muslims hold against the West, the other two being the Crusades and colonialism.

Theological understanding of Islam

From the above comparisons it is clear that it is impossible for a Christian to regard Muhammad as a legitimate prophet in line with the biblical revelation or to believe that his message was authentic revelation. It is alarming to note that the General Council of the United Church of Canada released a statement in 2006 that "acknowledges the prophetic witness of Muhammad."[55] Any statement of this kind, no matter how cunningly phrased, would be seen by Muslims as confirmation of their position.

Islam should therefore not be viewed as a brother monotheistic faith like Judaism with which Christians have a special relationship. The idea of three sibling "Abrahamic" faiths is an Islamic concept, not a Christian one. Rather Islam should be viewed in the same bracket as Christian heresies, Jehovah's Witnesses or Mormons. According to the Islamic tradition Abraham went to Mecca with Ishmael his son and there built the ka'ba, a tradition which is not supported by the Old Testament. It has been argued that the reason Muhammad drew Abraham into the Islamic faith he had founded was in order to de-legitimize the Jewish tribes in Arabia who refused to recognize Muhammad as a true prophet. The New Testament shows (Galatians 3) that the significance of Abraham for Christians is his faith and his role as the channel for the fulfillment of God's promises through Christ, Abraham's descendant. "If you belong to Christ, then you are Abraham's offspring, heirs according to the promise." (Galatians 3:29) To accept the Muslims' concept of three "Abrahamic" faiths is effectively to legitimize Muhammad's prophethood as the last in the line of Abrahamic prophets. It is also to agree with the Islamic teaching on replacement – Judaism was replaced by Christianity which was in turn replaced by Islam. The ultimate logic of this would be for all Christians to convert to Islam.

Christians must not let themselves forget the basic truth that it is faith **in Jesus Christ** which God is looking for, not faith in general. In a secular, materialistic culture, it is tempting to think that Muslims and Christians can be allies against the overwhelming godless hedonism which surrounds them both. For example, Philip Yancey says,

> Perhaps our day calls for a new kind of ecumenical movement: not of doctrine, not even of religious unity, but one that builds on what Jews, Christians, and Muslims hold in common, for the sake of mutual survival.[56]

But Christians must always bear in mind that Islam denies the heart of the Christian faith, and that its very creed – which resounds from minarets five times a day as the *muezzin* calls Muslims to prayer – was formulated to deny the deity of Christ and the finality of His revelation. When the *muezzin* calls "There is no god but God" he is saying that Jesus is not God, and when he adds that "Muhammad is his messenger" he is saying that Jesus has been superseded by Muhammad.

Issues

There are numerous issues related to Islam and especially its presence in the West which Christians should be aware of. Given that Islam does not separate the sacred from the secular or religion from society, the presence of Islam is bound to involve Islamic aspirations for the reconstruction of society according to Islamic values.

Under the guise of preventing Islamophobia, of fighting racism and of struggling for equal rights in a multiracial society, Islamic lobby groups in the West pressurize governments, parliaments, media, schools, academia and the legal systems of their adopted countries to move Western societies in the direction of expanding their Judeo-Christian basis to include Islam, thus creating a society with a Judeo-Christian-Islamic basis. From this point they move on gradually to seek for Islam privileges above any other religion or faith community. A stage in this process is the Warsaw Declaration of the Council of Europe, agreed in May 2005, where, as a result of Turkish lobbying, Islamophobia was for the first time listed alongside anti-Semitism as an example of religious intolerance and discrimination to be condemned and eradicated. No other kinds of religious discrimination were mentioned by name.

There is also an argument presented by some Muslim strategists that in order to avoid cultural conflicts the "moderate Muslims" and the "moderate Christians" should unite against the "extremists" in both camps. The suggestion is that both kinds of extremists are a danger to communal harmony. This is a very subtle twisting of issues, since it negates the huge difference between Muslim extremists (who call for the murder of unbelievers, and denounce freedom, democracy etc.) and conservative Christians (who do not do any of those things). The increasingly frequent phenomenon of equating fundamentalist Islam with fundamentalist Christianity is extremely misleading. Fundamentalist Christianity is ultimately based on love and on being conformed to Christ; it rejects the principle of violence, unlike fundamentalist Islam.

Legal protection

Some Western states have adopted legislation that seeks to protect religions (as opposed to their followers) by prohibiting incitement to religious hatred or the vilification of religion. This has in effect limited the freedom of expression so prized by Western democracies. Muslims are quick to seize upon any available legislation to try to attack any perceived slighting of Islam.

Italian journalist Oriana Fallaci (1929-2006) faced legal proceedings in Switzerland (2002), France (2003) and Italy (2005) for her book *La Rabbia e L'Orgoglio* (Rage and Pride) which warned of the danger posed by Islamism to Western civilization and freedoms and accepted the concept of a clash of cultures between Islam and the West. Her opponents included both Islamic groups and anti-racism groups.

In September 2002 Michel Houellebecq, a French philosopher, was taken to court by the Paris Mosque and the Muslim World League for incitement to racial hatred. In one of his novels he had depicted a woman being killed by Islamic terrorists. He had also described the Qur'an as appalling. The court cleared him of all charges on October 22, 2002, agreeing that his remarks were a judgment on a religion, not an incitement to hatred.

In the Australian state of Victoria, two Christian pastors were found guilty in December 2004 because they had made statements critical of Islam at a seminar intended for Christians. The complaints were made by the Islamic Council of Victoria under the state's Racial and Religious Tolerance Act (2001) and the section which the two pastors were found to have breached was a ban on inciting "hatred against, serious contempt for or revulsion or severe ridicule of" another person or group on the basis of religious belief or activity. The pastors appealed and the case was finally settled by mediation in 2007, but has left a legacy of intolerance, mistrust and fear in Victoria. It is ironic that this should be the result of a law which was intended to promote tolerance.

The United Nations has in recent years passed a number of resolutions on areas such as combating defamation of religion, intolerance or discrimination on the basis of religion. Some of these resolutions have specifically named Islam but no other faith as an example of a religion which needs to be protected. The Organization of the Islamic Conference has been active in pressing for the protection of Islam in this way.

In some Muslim states *shari'a*-based blasphemy and apostasy laws are used to intimidate Muslims in order to prevent them from expressing reformist and liberal ideas on Islam. Non-Muslims also are often prosecuted under these laws which carry harsh punishments. Following international Muslim protests over cartoons of Muhammad published in the West (see pages 69-70) the Organization of the Islamic Conference[57] called for the adoption of legislations to protect the sanctity of religions and prophets.

Education

Muslims are making use of Western education systems to present a favorable image of Islam to the West. Many of the Muslim educators and institutions approached by Western governments and public bodies for advice are influenced by Islamism; they will therefore present a sanitized view of Islam, ignoring elements deemed objectionable in the West, while sometimes denigrating and minimizing other Muslim streams they oppose.

In a process which might be called the Islamization of knowledge, Muslims are trying to influence school curricula and to gain input into the process of rewriting the textbooks used for religious education and history. A version of Islam is presented that ignores its more violent aspects and the historical atrocities committed in its name. The guidelines offered are also silent about the inferior position of women and non-Muslims in Islamic societies as outlined by *shari'a*.[58]

The climate of accusations of Islamophobia is making many teachers in the Europe and the US so anxious to avoid criticism that they are unable to teach an objective view of Islam. The result is a tendency to teach Islam more sympathetically than Christianity, so that school-children are studying Christianity from a critical basis but are often taught Islam completely uncritically. Some teaching methods include asking the students (even of primary school age) to pretend to be a Muslim and try to enter into a Muslim's thought processes. Young children are also being taken to visit mosques.[59]

Another significant trend is the installation of footbaths or foot-washing stations for Muslims on university campuses in the United States. Most notable was the University of Michigan-Dearborn's setting aside of $25,000 to install footbaths in restrooms on campus. This caused a public outcry over the use of taxpayer money for religious purposes. In August 2007, *The New York Times* reported that over a dozen universities across the United States had installed footbaths, or included them in new buildings.[60]

Another issue is that of Islamic schools, where Muslim children are taught a very strict, classical understanding of their faith. In

October 2007, a federal panel in the United States urged the State Department to shut down the Saudi Academy in Fairfax, Virginia, an outlying suburb of Washington, DC. The Academy is a private school owned and run by the Saudi government through its embassy in the Washington DC area. The Islamic Saudi Academy operates two campuses in Fairfax County, about which the U.S. Commission on International Religious Freedom expressed "significant concerns." According to *The Washington Post* the Commission contended that the Academy was "promoting a brand of religious intolerance that could prove a danger to the United States."[61] Another Islamic school in the United States was exposed as a center for extremism. The Khalil Gibran International Academy in New York presented itself as a place where children could learn Arabic, but it was later discovered to be providing an education in Islamist thinking.[62]

Treatment of women[63]

Some Muslim women (primarily of the secularized Western elites) enjoy equal status with men, but most suffer legal and cultural discrimination and restrictions on personal freedoms. This is especially severe in countries that operate *shari'a* courts in addition to the secular court system and even more so in countries which do not have civil/secular courts at all.[64] Women have fewer rights than men in divorce and custody cases. As mentioned above, the value of a woman's testimony in a law court is worth less than that of a man and she gets less compensation for the same injury. In some countries women need their husband's permission to work or to travel abroad. Child marriages, forced marriages, female genital mutilation, polygamy, rape, honor killings and violent abuse by husbands are still fairly widespread. Not every item in this list is part of classical Islam, but Islam's general attitude towards women creates a climate which allows the other abuses to flourish unchecked. While the Taliban regime in

Afghanistan was an extreme example of repression of women, UN and other human rights organizations have consistently reported on gross violations of the human rights of women in Muslim states.[65]

Some Muslim women are campaigning for a reinterpretation of *shari'a* rules on the status of women, but it is an uphill struggle which has made little impact so far. Ayaan Hirsi Ali, a Somali-born political scientist and former Dutch parliamentarian now living in the United States, had to go into hiding in 2002 after receiving a barrage of hate mail and death threats from Muslims following a live debate on Dutch TV in which she accused Islam of treating women shoddily, and conservative Muslim groups of covering up cases of domestic violence and child abuse. Ms Hirsi Ali also condemned the Dutch government's support for programs promoting multiculturalism which she claimed help keep Muslim women isolated from Dutch society.

It is striking that the cause of women in Islam has not been widely taken up in West. The traditional treatment of women and girls is perceived to be a part of Islamic culture and therefore above criticism, even if such treatment would be considered abuse in other contexts. The Sharia Council of Darul Uloom London has issued a set of rules on divorce and re-marriage which clearly envisage the possibility of pre-pubescent girls being married.[66] It is surprising that this has not provoked a furore, particularly amongst Western feminists and liberals. An encouraging sign, however, is that some secularized Muslim women themselves are no longer keeping silent but are speaking out about the discrimination women face under Islam and about the horror of female genital mutilation and so-called honor killings.

Implementation of *shari'a*

Western colonial rulers partially dismantled the *shari'a* establishment in many of the Muslim countries they governed, replacing it to some extent with Western-style codes of law. However, since independence, many Muslim states have reintroduced parts of *shari'a* or have even designated it a source of their legislation. In Saudi Arabia it is regarded as the constitution, while in Iran it is the sole source of the legal system. Muslim groups seeking the reform of *shari'a* have gradually been marginalized.

Whether or not *shari'a* is officially applied in any particular country at present, the long history of Muslims living under *shari'a* has ensured that the attitudes behind it are still prevalent amongst Muslims in all parts of the globe. The demand for the reintroduction of *shari'a* is a major platform of many Islamist movements. Even in the UK, US and other Western countries there is a creeping Islamization which amounts to a *de facto* application of *shari'a*. Examples in the UK include the introduction of *shari'a*-compliant mortgages and pensions, and the provision of *halal* food in schools, prisons and hospitals. The Metropolitan Police now permit Muslim police officers to wear turbans. There have been calls for the legalization of polygamy, this being presented as a basic human right for Muslim men. A London-based Sharia Council has already been mentioned and this is only one of many *shari'a* councils and *shari'a* courts operating informally in the UK to deal with divorce and other family disputes for the Muslim community.[67]

A similar situation is developing in the United States. *The Wall Street Journal Online* reported in 2007 that Islamists were "piggy-backing on our civil rights laws… to move slowly toward a two-tier legal system" and described several relevant events over the previous four years.[68] For example, taxi drivers at the Minneapolis-St. Paul airport began refusing customers who were carrying alcohol. Then in June 2006, the local Muslim American Society issued a *fatwa* prohibiting drivers from carrying alcohol. The Metropolitan Airports Commission proposed a two color top-light project, to indicate which drivers would accept passengers with alcohol, but this was later rejected. Had this passed it would have marked the first time a US government agency formally recognized *shari'a*. Some taxi drivers also refused to take blind passengers with guide dogs or passengers with other pets. According to airport officials, in the five years to January 2007, 5,400 passengers were turned away by taxi drivers either for carrying alcohol or for having an animal with them. Similarly some Muslim cashiers at Twin Cities Target stores now refuse to scan any products containing pork and insist that other cashiers handle the items, or even that customers scan them for themselves.

Shari'a-compliant mortgages in the US first began in the year 2000 through Fannie Mae. In response to requests from the New York office of the United Bank of Kuwait asking for Islamic residential finance products to be allowed as "functionally equivalent" arrangements, the Office of Comptroller of the Currency Administrator of National Banks (OCC) issued "Interpretive Letters" in December 1997 and November 1999.[69]

In June 2004, the US Treasury Department appointed Mahmoud A. El-Gamal as its principal adviser and scholar-in-residence on Islamic finance. The Treasury felt that with the growth in Islamic finance in the US, a deeper understanding of the issues concerned was a top priority.[70] El-Gamal is the author of Islamic Society of North America (ISNA) manual of Islamic finance.

In the UK, the Islamic financial market flourishes with support from business and popular media, and aided by the sympathy and enthusiasm of Prime Minister Gordon Brown who expressed his eagerness to make London the world hub for the *shari'a*-compliant finance when he was Chancellor.

The resurgence of Islam has been accompanied by greatly increased violence against non-Muslims in countries like Sudan, Nigeria and Indonesia. This results from a revival of the *shari'a* concepts of *jihad* in its military sense and of the inferiority of non-Muslims.

The spread of rule by *shari'a* is without doubt part of the Islamist global strategy. One of the regions where this is being most actively pursued at present is sub-Saharan Africa, where Christianity and Islam are both growing rapidly. The introduction of *shari'a* effectively stakes a claim to Muslim superiority as opposed to Christian demands for the equality of all before the law. It also opens the door to the possibility of a Muslim minority taking control of the state, while shaping all of society in an Islamic mould.

To allow Muslims in the West to be different in culture is one thing. To derive from this "right of difference" that they also have the right to be ruled by a different set of laws is unacceptable, since this would lead to the disintegration of the state and ultimately to the "Balkanization" of Western society.

Media and freedom of speech

Islam typically rejects any kind of negative comment and seeks to protect itself from criticism. In Pakistan the crime of "defiling the name of Muhammad" is seen as blasphemy and carries a mandatory death sentence. In 2005 a chemistry teacher at a school in Saudi Arabia was sentenced to 40 months in prison and 750 lashes because he spoke against jihadist violence, made fun of Muslim clerics' beards, and "favored" Christians and Jews. In Egypt any criticism of Muhammad or the religion itself, no matter how scholarly, tends to be interpreted as apostasy and brings dire punishment. For example, Professor Nasr Hamid Abu-Zayd was declared an apostate by the Cairo Appeals Court in June 1995 and, as an apostate, was ordered to separate from his wife. (Dissolution of the marriage is one of the classical Islamic penalties for apostasy in addition to the death sentence.) The professor and his wife fled the country together.

Abu-Zayd is a liberal-secularist academic who had held the chair of Islamic and Arabic Studies at Cairo University. In the course of his research he had studied the Qur'an and *hadith*; he had called the Qur'an a linguistic text, described it as a cultural product and denied its pre-existence on a tablet in heaven. In Sudan Mahmoud Muhammad Taha was executed for apostasy on January 20, 1985 because he refused to repent of his liberal views of Islam; he had been given just three days to repent, in accordance with *shari'a* rules.

Fearful of giving offence or being accused of Islamophobia, some sections of the Western media succumbed to a form of self-censorship in which Islam could not be criticized. Recently, however, it appears the pendulum may be swinging back the other way, with a growing willingness to express negative comments about certain aspects of Islam.

Muslim media in the West tend to blame Christianity for promoting colonialism, secularism and immorality as well as for being irrational and obscurantist. Christianity is presented as an ally of Orientalism and Judaism, which are considered by many Muslims to be engaged in a struggle to demean and destroy Islam.[71] Where left-wing anti-Christian attitudes, guilt for colonialism, political correctness and post-modern relativism predominate, it is easy for Muslim lobbyists to have considerable influence. Secular commentators often tend to denigrate Christianity but to put Islam on a pedestal. An idealized Islam is presented and compared to the many shortcomings of real-life Christianity.

It is noticeable also that blasphemies against the Lord Jesus Christ are a daily occurrence in the media, whereas the name of Muhammad is rarely mistreated, indeed it is increasingly prefixed with the title "The Prophet."[72] Muhammad is respected but Christ is reviled.

On September 30, 2005 a leading Danish daily newspaper, *Jyllands-Posten*, published twelve cartoons of Muhammad, including one in which he was shown wearing a turban shaped like a bomb with a burning fuse. A Danish Muslim leader, Imam Ahmed Abu-Laban, said the cartoons were inflicting mental torture on Muslims because they were blasphemous and insulting to Islam. The editor who commissioned the cartoons did so as a response to the self-censorship which he said had overtaken Europe since Dutch film-maker Theo van Gogh was murdered in 2004 by a radical Muslim for making a film critical of Islam's treatment of women. He wanted to test whether people would censor themselves for fear of provoking Muslims. Under the leadership of Egypt and Saudi Arabia, outraged Muslims across the world protested, as did ambassadors from Muslim countries, Arab foreign ministers, and the Organization of the Islamic Conference. By early 2006 Muslims were rioting and attacking Christian minorities and Western embassies. Protests were also received from the United Nations, the Council of Europe and the European Union. Would any of these have protested about a blasphemous depiction of the Lord Jesus Christ or indeed of a Hindu deity?

Politics

In Islam politics forms an integral part of religion and must serve the goal of protecting and promoting Islam, extending its dominion and implementing *shari'a* as far as possible. At the local and national level, Muslims in the West are carefully and patiently working to gain political power. In Germany radical Muslims are urging other Muslims to acquire German citizenship so that they will be eligible to vote. They would like a Muslim presence in all political parties so that they can maximize their influence on the German political scene. In Britain, where many Muslims are from the Indian sub-continent, the strong clan networks known as *biraderis* make it easy for Muslim candidates to gain "block votes". The candidate's party allegiance or electoral platform is of virtually no relevance, as their entire *biraderi* will vote for them anyway because loyalty to the *biraderi* takes precedence.

As already noted, Muslim states have set up international organizations such as the Organization of the Islamic Conference and the Muslim World League to coordinate global Muslim political goals, attitudes and responses. These also fund and direct a vast worldwide missionary (*da'wa*) effort.

Cruel *shari'a* punishments

According to *shari'a*, law courts must impose mandatory prescribed punishments (*hudud*, singular *hadd*) for certain specific crimes claimed to be committed against God and his rights. These include theft, highway robbery, adultery and fornication, false accusation of adultery and fornication, and drinking alcohol. Some Muslims also include apostasy from Islam as a *hadd* crime. In these cases the judge has no discretion in his sentencing, as the punishments are laid down in the Qur'an or *hadith*.

Although there are four main schools of Sunni *shari'a* law with slight differences between them, the following list of punishments is generally accepted:

- Theft: amputation of the hand at the wrist for a first offence. Further amputations follow for further offences.
- Highway robbery: loss of hands and feet. If the highway robbery involves murder, then the death sentence is imposed.
- Adultery: stoning to death
- Fornication by an unmarried person: 100 lashes
- False accusation of adultery or fornication: 80 lashes
- Drinking alcohol: 40 lashes
- Apostasy: death

While the severity of the punishments is theoretically tempered by strict rules of evidence, this has not stopped them being practiced in certain modern states, for example, Saudi Arabia, Iran, Sudan, parts of Nigeria and Somalia, and Afghanistan when it was under Taliban rule.

Dhimmi

It cannot be denied that *shari'a* discriminates against non-Muslims, granting to Jews and Christians an inferior second-class status as *dhimmi*; this might be termed "institutional injustice." *Dhimmi* are often described as "protected," because they are allowed to keep their faith and yet live. Other non-Muslims would, according to classical Islam, have to convert to Islam or be killed.

But *dhimmi*, although allowed to live, were not according to classical Islam entitled to equal status with Muslims. A host of rules and regulations affected their daily life, e.g. clothes, transport and places of worship. The thrust of these rules was to mark out the *dhimmi* visibly as non-Muslims, to show that they were considered inferior to Muslims, and to curtail their religious activities so that they did not impinge on the consciousness of the Muslim majority. This treatment of Jews and Christians is often described by Muslims as "tolerance;" it is important to realize that this does not imply equality or respect. A special poll tax called *jizya* was required from *dhimmi*. It was handed over with a humiliating public ceremony, in accordance with the teachings of the Qur'an that Jews and Christians should "pay the *jizya* with willing submission, and feel themselves subdued."[73]

While the full *dhimmi* system is not formally implemented by any modern Muslim-majority state, the legacy of hundreds of years of official scorn and discrimination towards non-Muslims has left its mark on most Muslim societies in terms of an enduring popular prejudice against non-Muslims. This is the reason for much of the injustice suffered by Christian minorities in Muslim countries. It is the reason that so often police, judiciary, media, employers and teachers – not to mention angry mobs – can get away with anti-Christian behavior, for the majority of society feels deep down that this is right and proper, part of God's plan for his creation.

In some countries there are even the remains of certain *dhimmi* regulations within twenty-first century legal systems. Islamic law courts function in some countries and these have an inbuilt bias against non-Muslims (and against women). In traditional Islamic law, the number of witnesses on each side of the case plays an important part in deciding the verdict. But Islam states that the testimony of a Christian is worth less than that of a Muslim. (Likewise, the testimony of a woman is worth less than that of a man.) So if a case hinges on the word of one Muslim against the word of one Christian, the Muslim must automatically be believed. This makes Christians very vulnerable when tried in Islamic courts.

The same mindset can also affect cases in non-Islamic courts, for example, when a Christian is accused by a Muslim under Pakistan's notorious "blasphemy law." Many malicious accusations have been made by Muslims against innocent Christians. The accuser knows that there is a mandatory death sentence for "defiling" the name of Muhammad but no penalty at all for false accusation. The accuser also knows that, as a Muslim, his words may be believed in preference to those of the Christian defendant.

A similar sliding scale governs the payment of compensation for injuries or death. In classical Islam, an injury suffered by a Christian (or a woman) receives a lower sum than the same injury suffered by a Muslim (or a man). Iranian Christians rejoiced in 2003 when for the first time a court granted the family of a murdered Christian as much compensation as would be given to the family of a murdered Muslim. Previously non-Muslims in Iran received only a fraction of what Muslims were entitled to.

Apostasy

For most contemporary Muslims across the spectrum of beliefs and ideologies, apostasy from Islam still carries shocking associations as an abhorrent sin. Theologically in Islam this is one of the few sins God cannot forgive. Even for some modernists and secularists apostasy has negative connotations of betrayal of one's community and rejection of one's heritage. This explains why so few Muslim voices are ever raised in defense of those accused of apostasy.

In Islamic jurisprudence, apostasy (*irtidad*) is linked to unbelief, blasphemy and heresy (all combined under the term *kufr*), which are sometimes used interchangeably. All are regarded as serious crimes, but there is unanimous consensus in all schools of *shari'a* that apostasy by a sane, adult male Muslim is punishable by death. Three out of five main versions of *shari'a* also have the death penalty for women converts; the other two schools specify that the women should be imprisoned until they return to Islam. In practice the death penalty is not often implemented nowadays, but it is common to deprive apostates of their civil rights (the *shari'a* has detailed regulations for this kind of punishment for apostates, in addition to the death penalty). Even where there are no official penalties, those who leave Islam are more than likely to suffer harassment or rejection from family and community, sometimes even death.

Muslims too can be accused of unbelief, blasphemy and heresy and even apostasy if their beliefs are not mainstream. This is often what happens to liberals espousing a modernization of the Islamic faith. (See pages 68-69 for examples in Egypt and Sudan.) They may then be punished, murdered by zealous Islamists or even executed by the state. A significant feature of accusations of apostasy and blasphemy in Muslim-majority countries is the way they are often uncritically accepted as true by members of the police and judiciary, with little or no evidence required beyond the word of their accuser.

Jihad and the extension of Islamic territory

Calls for *jihad* in the sense of physical violence have been increasing with the growth of the Islamist movement. All Islamic terrorist groups justify their actions from the classical theology of *jihad*. They regard as permanent and literal the Qur'anic commands to fight Jews and Christians until they submit to Islamic dominance. Secular Muslim regimes are regarded as infidel for failing fully to implement *shari'a* and are therefore likewise to be fought by *jihad* until they are replaced by truly Islamic governments. Osama bin Laden's al-Qa'eda group and many similar organizations are inspired by this understanding of *jihad*.

In the West non-violent methods are being used to seek to gain Islamic sovereignty over geographical areas. The implementation of *shari'a* in family matters and Muslim involvement in politics have already been mentioned. The extension of sacred space in the sense of the sanctification of physical territory is also seen in the name-changes forced by some British Muslims in the London Borough of Tower Hamlets who objected to saints' names and other Christian-sounding names in their area for parks, electoral wards etc.

Sufi Muslims may also "take" territory spiritually by means of a religious procession (*julus*) in which the name of Allah is chanted in various short phrases. The chanting (*dhikr*) is characteristic of Sufism. "This chanting not only purifies their hearts and souls, but also sacralizes and 'Islamizes' the very earth, the buildings, the streets and neighborhoods through which they march." Such processions are held twice a year in certain British cities including Birmingham, Manchester and London. They are also held in North America, for example, in Toronto and New York.[74,75]

Christian-Muslim Relations

Having clarified the relationship between Christianity and Islam theologically and spiritually, and having highlighted some of the most pressing contemporary issues for Christians concerned about Islam, how are Christians actually to interact with and relate to Muslims?

Building friendships

A number of stumbling blocks and complications make the task of building friendships with Muslims rather more difficult than with other non-Christians. Christians may be puzzled or bewildered by the apparently capricious way in which Muslims relate to them. But often there is a theological rationale behind the Muslims' actions and reactions.

Many Muslims consider that it is displeasing to God for them to have Christians as friends. This is based on a verse in the Qur'an (sura 5, verse 51):

> O you who believe! Take not the Jews and the Christians as Auliya'
> (friends, protectors, helpers), they are but Auliya' of each other.
> And if any amongst you takes them (as Auliya'), then surely, he is
> one of them.

There is a *hadith* which even forbids Muslims from greeting Christians, but fortunately there are few Muslims who take this literally.

> Allah's Messenger (peace be upon him) said: Do not greet the Jews and

the Christians before they greet you and when you meet any one of them on the roads force him to go to the narrowest part of it.[76]

The antipathy for Christians is reinforced by the fact that faithful Muslims who pray five times daily will, in the course of their prayers, repeat seventeen times a day in Arabic the first sura of the Qur'an, known as the *fatiha*, which is regarded as the most important sura in the whole Qur'an. The sixth and seventh verses of the *fatiha* run:

> Guide us to the Straight Way. The Way of those on whom You have bestowed Your Grace, not (the way) of those who earned Your Anger (such as the Jews), nor of those who went astray (such as the Christians).

Although the Arabic does not contain the words in brackets, these are added to the English translation to show Muslims how they should interpret this text according to the guidance of the *hadith*, i.e. they are supposed to think of Jews as those who have earned God's anger and Christians as those who have gone astray. Such a message, repeated seventeen times a day, does not make for easy friendships with non-Muslims.

Kafirun

Those outside the *umma* tend to be despised and rejected as thoroughly as those inside the *umma* are embraced. A non-Muslim is a *kafir* (plural *kafirun* or *kuffar*). It is hard to convey in English the gross insult conveyed by this technical term. Translating it as "infidel" conveys something of the nuance of "enemy" but still lacks the abusive quality.

The habitual use by many Muslims in conversation with each other of the word *kafir* for "non-Muslim" serves to reinforce an attitude of contempt towards non-Muslims. Even though Sir Iqbal Sacranie, secretary-general of the Muslim Council of Britain, has told British Muslims not to use this term, it is for many normal usage. Dr Taj Hargey has said that it is heard ad infinitum and ad nauseam. It's there. It's with us. We see it from the time you're a child, you're given this idea that those people they are kafir, they're unbelievers. They are not equal to you. They are different from you. You are superior to them because you have the truth, they don't have the truth ... So we have this from a very young age.[77]

The barrier caused by the use of the word "*kafir*" might be compared with the greater barrier to friendship with Pakistanis for white Britons who normally call them "Pakis" compared with white Britons who normally use more respectful vocabulary. In the United States racial epithets convey similar disdain and, in some cases, assert the superiority of one group over another. The term *kafir* is just as harsh and grievous.

Gifts and hospitality

Hospitality and the exchange of gifts are two of the linchpins of relationships in the East (and have importance in the West as well). But what happens when Christians try to do this with conservative Muslims? Often they will find that they are warmly welcomed into the Muslim home and plied with delicious food, but cannot persuade the Muslims to make a return visit to the Christian home. If conservative Muslims do come to visit the Christians, they may refuse any form of refreshment. This is more than just concern about eating non-*halal* food as there are plenty of Islamically acceptable kinds of food which can be offered. Two factors are the cultural concept of Christians as religiously "unclean" (arising from the discriminatory laws against them in the *shari'a*) and the fact that accepting a meal means owing a favor to the host. In addition, there are *hadiths* recording Muhammad's disapproval of pictures, which are commonly found in Western homes. For example:

> Abu Talha, a companion of Allah's Apostle and one of those who fought at the Badr together with Allah's Apostle told me

that Allah's Apostle said, "Angels do not enter a house in which there is a dog or a picture." He meant the images of creatures that have souls.[78]

As Muslims in the West become more religiously observant, they are growing less willing to enter Christian homes. Furthermore, since dogs are considered "unclean", as suggested in the *hadith* above, and contact with a dog would make a Muslim unclean, many Muslims will try to avoid entering a home where there is a dog.

With regard to gifts, Muslims will often be generous givers but reluctant to receive. The local imam may bestow a beautiful copy of the Qur'an on the local minister but brush aside the Bible which he is offered in return. This was the experience of the Bishop of Hildesheim, Germany, who was warmly welcomed to the mosque by the imam. The imam presented the grateful bishop with a Qur'an but rejected with horror the Bible which the bishop tried to present to him in return.[79]

Muslims are always on the alert for opportunities for mission, such as giving Qur'ans to non-Muslims. But they guard themselves against anything that might serve to deflect them from the way of Islam, such as the scriptures of another faith. A *fatwa* issued in April 2008 by a South African *mufti* gave guidance to a worried Muslim in the United Arab Emirates who had accepted a Bible given to him at his workplace because he had felt he could not refuse. The *fatwa* advised him to pass the Bible on to a Muslim scholar in the field of comparative religion, who would be able to use it as a reference work "for the sake of countering the beliefs of modern-day Christianity for the purpose of giving Da'wah to Islam."[80]

Many Muslims feel they would be sinning if they even touched a copy of the Bible. A Muslim worker in a major retailer in the UK refused to serve a customer purchasing a children's book of Bible stories because she said it was "unclean."[81]

A book of instructions for new converts to Islam tells them the attitude they should have to the Bible:

> The previously divinely revealed books have suffered a great deal of distortion, additions and deletions, as Allah has mentioned in the Qur'an. Therefore it is not allowed for Muslims to read or look at them. The exception is if the person is well-grounded in knowledge and desires to show what has occurred in them of distortions and contradictions.[82]

On the other hand, Muslims who are seeking a spiritual reality and have not found it in Islam may be immensely grateful to receive a Bible or a DVD of the Jesus film. Christians should not refrain from offering such materials, which are often the means by which Muslims become Christians, but should understand the possibility of their gift being rejected.

Places of worship

Exchange visits between the local church and the local mosque might seem to some a good way to foster Christian-Muslim relations. Even better, it might seem, would be inviting Muslims to share in the leading of Christian worship or Christian celebrations. However, for Christians who seek to follow the teaching of the Bible, this would be not just compromise but bordering on apostasy.

Muslim leaders will probably be much happier to accept a Christian invitation to the church than an invitation to a private home. Sometimes the initial suggestion of the visit to the church may even come from the Muslims. Typically the pattern is that the imam preaches in the church and the minister merely prays in the mosque. This is seen by the Muslims as a victory for them. As in the attempted exchange of scriptures, the Muslims will use every opportunity to promote their faith and to prevent the similar promotion of Christianity.

In the widely distributed documentary film "Three Faiths, One God: Judaism, Christianity, Islam" (2005, Auteur Productions) Muslim leaders such as Imam Yahya Hendi, the Muslim Chaplain of Georgetown University in Washington, DC, are shown preaching in Christian pulpits and leading a group of Christian children in Islamic prayers. Christian leaders such as Bishop John Chane of the Episcopal Diocese of Washington, DC, and others meanwhile are seen throughout the documentary speaking to an interviewer or an interfaith audience about the truth and beauty of Islam, and what they describe as "similarities between scriptural texts and religious practices" in "the Abrahamic religions."[83] This documentary has been shown on public television stations (PBS) in the United States, publicly screened at official events such as one convened by the US Department of State,[84] and used in various church and interfaith settings.

It is striking how one-sided these "exchanges" often are. It seems that Christians are expected to do all the learning and Muslims all the teaching. Christians involved in any such initiatives should strive to ensure there is a level playing field with both Christians and Muslims able to share their faith as well as to listen to what the others have to say.

It is mystifying why some church leaders seem to endorse an asymmetrical kind of relationship by inviting Muslims to share their faith from a church pulpit without ensuring that there is a reciprocal opportunity for Christians to share their faith with Muslims. David Gillett, Anglican Bishop of Bolton and co-chair of the Christian- Muslim Forum in England, suggests five ways to develop relationships with Muslims in the UK, starting with "How many of us have invited a Muslim to speak to our congregation about their faith?"[85] Many Christians would want to plead with Bishop Gillett not to promote Christian-Muslim relations by having

Islam preached to Christians, given that Islam not only contradicts the Christian faith but furthermore calls for the killing of any Muslim who becomes a Christian. They would ask him to find a more neutral and balanced way of developing good relationships without such a one-sided dominance of one faith over the other. Ultimately, biblical truth must take precedence over both political pragmatism and good community race and interfaith relations. Those who do not discern this may find themselves unwittingly on the road towards apostasy.

Muslim leadership in Christian events is a very different matter from inviting Muslim individuals to be part of the congregation at Christian worship. Stephen Lowe, Bishop of Hulme, urges Christians in Manchester, UK, to invite Muslims to tell Christians about their faith, to organize joint Christian/Muslim school assemblies, and to replace an annual "June Whit Walk" (a celebration of the Christian Whitsun) every other year with a joint Christian- Muslim "Walk of Faiths."

> One of the best days of the year for me was the June Whit Walks where it was a privilege for me to walk alongside the Muslim Lord Mayor of Manchester and the Mayor of Salford on what is at heart a Christian celebration.
>
> **Why not every other year make this into a Walk of Faiths with us celebrating together through the streets of Manchester what we share rather than what divides us? What a witness to the city and Greater Manchester about our unity in a divided and broken world.**[86]

Few Muslim leaders would dream of compromising their faith for the sake of the feelings of Christians or to show inter-religious solidarity, so it is hard to understand why Bishop Lowe wants to turn opportunities for Christian witness into opportunities to promote the

Islamic faith, effectively neutralizing the Christian message. Further-more, the "editing" of the Christian faith could well be interpreted by Muslims as acceptance of the superiority of Islam. A situation that sometimes arises is that a request is made by Muslims who have no mosque building of their own to use the church premises for their Friday prayers. It may seem the act of a good neighbor to say yes, especially if the church is not used at Friday lunchtimes. But the issue of the Muslim attitude to territory (see pages 25, 75) must be considered, as well as the reality of the spiritual dimension and in particular the possibility of cursing prayers (see pages 41-43). Even when curses are not being prayed, the normal Islamic creed, which is recited whenever Muslims pray, specifically denies the truth of the Christian Gospel with its words "There is no god but God, and Muhammad is the apostle of God". (See page 55.) Should a church building be the scene of such anti-Christian affirmations? Another factor to take into account is the message which this dual use of the church sends to the local community that "Islam and Christianity are one and the same."

In the light of this it is probably best not to use either church buildings or mosques for Christian-Muslim encounters, but to use a neutral venue.

New mosques

Another difficult issue for Christians comes when Muslims seek to build a mosque in their local area. In a liberal Western democracy this might seem at first glance to be a non-issue – surely it is only fair to allow them their own place of worship, indeed to facilitate their application for planning permission? By the same reasoning, Christians might feel that it would be showing the love of Christ to assist Muslims in their mosque-building project, for example, by raising funds. But there are implications which should be weighed carefully.

Firstly, there is the issue of religious territoriality, not only the ideology and spirituality but also the practicality. A mosque building consolidates and strengthens the Muslim community, both psychologically and physically. It simultaneously weakens any outreach efforts that churches may have been making in the area to, say, Muslim youngsters through church youth clubs. Questions should be asked about whether the size of the building is proportional to the number of Muslims in the area. Another question is the size of the building compared with the nearest church (which may turn out to be surprisingly near). Muslims often make a point of building a mosque close to a church and taller than the church – an illustration in bricks and mortar of their superiority. Christians may feel that it is unchristian to compete for visible status in this way, but they should at least be aware of how local Muslims will be thinking, both now and in the future. Another important point concerns the theological persuasion of the mosque – will it encourage radicalism? Finally, on the issue of fairness and justice, it is valid to lift one's gaze from the local community and pan around to consider places of worship worldwide. There are many Muslim-majority contexts where Christians find it difficult to get permission for sufficient church buildings. This happens in countries which are popular holiday destinations for Westerners, for example, Malaysia and Egypt. In Saudi Arabia no church buildings are allowed at all. Could there be an argument for trying somehow to negotiate for reciprocal permission for Christian minorities in Muslim contexts before allowing Muslim minorities in the West to build as many mosques as they want?

Rt. Rev. James Jones, Anglican Bishop of Liverpool, UK, and an evangelical, has agreed to be patron of refurbishing a local mosque. His decision was based on the commandment "Love your neighbor." He also hoped to set an example of support and respect for religious minorities. The question arises as to how he can lend his name to support a place of worship for a faith which contradicts the message of the Bible. It is doubtful whether he would accept an invitation to be the patron of any other non-Christian place of worship, such as a Mormon temple, and therefore difficult to understand why he makes an exception for Islam.

Joining in Islamic worship

Sometimes Christians seek to develop good relations with Muslims by sharing in Islamic spiritual disciplines. These well-meant and often sacrificial gestures must be considered with great caution. For example, some Christians fast alongside Muslims during Ramadan. But what does this mean in the spiritual realm? The spiritual highlight of Ramadan is the "Night of Power" which marks the date on which Muhammad received the first revelation of the Qur'an.[87] Can a Christian really be involved in celebrating something which so profoundly contradicts the Gospel? Some Christians join in with Muslim prayers, for example, when breaking daily the Ramadan fast or when starting the fast again each morning. While there is no problem with a Christian praying the simple prayer before breaking the fast, it is very different situation if a Christian joins in the prayers before starting the fast. The latter prayers involve reciting both the creed and the *fatiha*, and a Christian saying these words would effectively be denying their faith. Christian-Muslim relations should be free of "Christian sentimentality" and of a *dhimmi*-like spirit of submission and appeasement on the part of the Christians. Blurring the boundaries does not help the relationship. As between neighbors in a street, clear boundaries lead to better relationships.

"Dialogue"

Within the Western Church, and particularly among evangelicals, there is increasing debate over how to "dialogue" with Muslims. Western Christians have a growing awareness of the need to understand Islam and Muslims, to foster relations, seek tolerance, and find effective common ground for working towards increasing peace.

However, much of the contemporary debate in the Western Church focuses on practical issues of how to relate to Muslims, which seem the most pressing and thus more important than how to understand Islam and its contemporary expressions, which is often lost or left unexamined.

When one hears of interfaith "dialogue" initiatives between Christian leaders and Muslim leaders what is usually meant is debate and discussion, perhaps on a particular area of mutual concern. This approach has some inherent risks, the first of which is the ambiguity of the term "dialogue."[88] The New Testament term *dialegomai*, as used of Paul (Acts 17:17) means argument with a view of convincing the listener. For Paul, dialogue was a form of evangelism. Paul did not gather the pagan religious leaders together for a round table discussion on religious commonalities and for mutual enrichment. Rather he argued with them to try to convince them (Acts 17:22-31). Paul had a burning desire to lead people to an encounter with the crucified and risen Lord.

However, most Christians involved in dialogue have no intention of persuading the Muslims with whom they are speaking to become Christians, wishing only to find areas of common ground on which all can agree. They approach such meetings simply as conversations, rather than as dialogue in the New Testament sense. There are only a small number of Christians who use dialogue as a starting-point for evangelism. It might be better, therefore, to describe such encounters more accurately and neutrally, perhaps as "discussion meetings."

On the other hand, Muslims will normally seize any opportunity to advance the cause of Islam, and that would include using dialogue initiatives to try to convert Christians. Sura 29, verse 46 of the Qur'an instructs Muslims:

> And argue not with the people of the Scriptures (Jews and Christians), unless it be in (a way) that is better (with good words and in good manner, inviting them to Islamic Monotheism with His Verses), except with such of them as do wrong: and say (to them): 'We believe in that which has been revealed to us and revealed to you; our Ilah (God) and your Ilah (God) is One (i.e. Allah), and to Him we have submitted (as Muslims).

A World Assembly of Muslim Youth (WAMY) study on *Christian Muslim Dialogue* demonstrates how Muslims should use dialogue opportunities to convince Christians of the superiority of the Qur'an to Christian scriptures. "Using the Holy Qur'an as standard… You can explain the Bible and correct the Jewish and Christian prejudice with the context of the Qur'an." The author asserts that the Qur'an, "the last revealed Book," can be used as the standard against which to judge other scriptures because it "has never been corrupted or adulterated." He cites sura 2, verse 2 and sura 15, verse 9 which speak of the reliability of the Qur'an's contents, while in contrast "all the other holy books (Torah, Psalms, Gospels, etc.) have been adulterated in the form of additions, deletions or alterations from the original."[89] The argument that the Muslim holy book is the "last revealed" of all the holy books is very important to Muslims as a reason for the superiority of their religion over others. It thus has implications for mission and conversion.[90]

It is ironic that the Muslims' understanding of "dialogue" is much more in line with Paul's than is that of most Christians. Muslims find it hard to believe that Christians are **not** seeking to convert them during the dialogue process; they cannot understand why Christians would not make use of this convenient opportunity for evangelism. As a result Muslims often suspect that such dialogue is a form of Christian deception.

Some of the other risks for Christians involved in such encounters are:

1. There is a likelihood that Christians will do all the giving and Muslims all the taking. This is inherent in the different nature of the two religions. As has already been seen, Christianity stresses meekness, humility, confession, repentance, sacrifice and self-denial. Islam prizes power, domination and honor. Muslims will usually present their case as victims, make accusations against Christianity and demand compensatory actions. At the same time they will fiercely resist any discussion of Muslim faults such as the bloody history of *jihad* (which they will usually deny) and the discriminatory treatment of Christians in Muslim contexts.

2. Key vocabulary is understood differently by Muslims and Christians, so there is a great risk of misunderstanding and of talking at cross purposes. For example, the word "peace" for Muslims carries the connotation of establishing peace and order by spreading Islamic rule and authority across the globe.[91] Similarly, when Muslims claim that Islamic societies were historically tolerant of non-Muslims, they mean that the non- Muslims were not killed, expelled or forcibly converted. This is very different from the modern Western understanding of tolerance as implying full equality of status and rights. Other words which can carry different meanings and connotations are "equality" itself, "self-defense," "terrorism," "innocent," "fasting" and "Holy Spirit" to name but a few.

3. Some Muslims consider any interaction with Christians as a justification for the use of *taqiyya* (dissimulation) in the cause

of Islam. As has been seen, some also hold that it is permissible for Muslims to break agreements made with non-Muslims. So any undertakings or pledges made by the Muslim side cannot necessarily be relied on, nor can any factual information given be automatically accepted as true.

Bearing in mind all these factors, it is very difficult to ensure that formal Christian-Muslim discussions do not become simply a search for the lowest common denominator, in which much that is essential to each religion is downplayed or – more often – completely ignored. Discussion of this kind – which is lacking to a greater or lesser degree in honesty, integrity, transparency or truth – may promote short-term peace of a kind. But unless it tackles the real issues of society and seeks with honesty and openness to develop methods of living together and addressing the treatment of minorities on both sides, the process will ultimately be futile.

The outrageous injustices suffered by Christian minorities in the Muslim world must not be forgotten by Western Christians involved in discussion with Muslims in the West. If they are not raised in discussion, then those minorities will have been betrayed by their Christian brothers and sisters in the West; they will have been sacrificed for the sake of peace on Western streets.

It is adding insult to injury when Western Christians "dialogue" with Muslim authorities in Muslim countries without involving the national Christians. Christians in the West should help and strengthen the national Churches in Muslim countries, who are in an extremely vulnerable position. Western Churches should take care to avoid finding themselves in a position where they are dialoguing with the Muslims and have bypassed the national Church. This is to treat the national Christians as if they were children, lacking the wisdom or ability to speak to their Muslim compatriots.

Furthermore, a test of "genuine" encounter would be whether both

Christian and Muslim partners are willing to accept converts speaking on the other side. All too often, Muslims involved in dialogue will include white converts to Islam but Christians from a Muslim background will not be allowed to participate on behalf of Christians.

A very high profile example of Christian-Muslim dialogue occurred in 2007-8 beginning with the release of a formal public letter ("A Common Word Between Us and You") organized by the Royal Aal al-Bayt Institute for Islamic Thought, Jordan and signed by 138 Muslim clerics. The October 13, 2007 open letter was sent to Christian leaders throughout the world.[92]

The following month, on November 18, 2007, Christian scholars and church leaders, largely from the United States, responded en masse via a full-page advertisement in *The New York Times*. The letter, titled "Loving God and Neighbor Together: A Christian Response to 'A Common Word Between Us and You,'" was drafted by evangelical Christians at the Yale Center for Faith and Culture, and signed by more than 300 Christians leaders, a great majority of whom were Western evangelicals.[93] However, there were many other Christians who rejected the Yale Center statement for its theological ambiguity and for naively and uncritically following the agenda set by the Muslims. Some of the Yale signatories later withdrew their signatures. While the writers of the Yale statement were surely confident of their theology, it could be said that they were behaving like *dhimmi*, bending over backwards to please the Muslims. Such "theological pragmatism" will only make Christians ridiculous in the eyes of the Muslims they dialogue with. For Muslims will think the Christians either do not take their own faith seriously, or are engaging in "Christian *taqiyya*," or are seeking to appease the Muslims because they are afraid. (A detailed analysis of the Yale Center statement is given in the Appendix, pages 118-145.)

Western governments are increasingly using "dialogue" as a method for tackling the ideological war between Islam and the

West. In other words, they are seeking to use the Church as a way of engaging the Muslim world in order to neutralize theologies of violence, promote tolerance, and establish cooperative relationships and ventures. The danger is that this practice will reinforce amongst Muslims their erroneous belief that all Western nations are ideologically Christian, and hence justify the persecution of Christian minorities in Muslim countries by radical Islamist groups. This politicization of the Church for Western political interests is reminiscent of the colonial period and is likely to have dire consequences for the Church in the Muslim world today. It could also diminish the effectiveness of the Western Church with regard to its witness to Muslim minorities in the West.

Christian-Muslim cooperation on non-religious projects

It is sometimes argued that it is good for Christians and Muslims to seek areas of common concern where they can work together. Such areas would include protecting the traditional family, anti-abortion issues, ecology, and relief of poverty. The logic behind this suggestion is that both Christians and Muslims share a common society and must seek to advance the common good. In such common ventures, there can be a lack of understanding on the Christians' part regarding possible Muslim aims; it is important that the Christians should first gain a realistic knowledge of the nature of Islam, its agenda and how Muslims view their relationship with Christians.

Traditionally there have been two viewpoints about Christians working with other groups to achieve social change. The first is to avoid working with non-Christians and simply to trust God and believe that he will work through Christian believers. The second is to work with like-minded people who are motivated by Christian principles whether or not they are committed Christians. A good example of the second is William Wilberforce and the abolition of the slave trade in the British Empire.

Today, however, the second position is being broadened to include those of other faiths, particularly Muslims. The question arises as to why the limit should be drawn at adherents of world faiths. Why not include Mormons and Jehovah's Witnesses, or people of goodwill who are humanists and atheists? These would be just as capable of engaging in good works motivated by good values. Careful thought should be given to defining the boundaries of those we can work with. Great confusion can be caused by emphasizing faith groups as if they have values in common not shared by people without faith, or as if all faiths share the same values as the Christian faith. This sends a message that all faiths are fundamentally the same. Where it is needful to engage in common causes – and this is becoming increasingly necessary in today's world – should not our aim be to work with people of goodwill (whether they have a faith or not) rather than specifically with people of faith e.g. Muslims? It is hard to find any warrant in the Bible for interfaith cooperation. In fact it can be argued that cooperation with other faiths actually led to the decline of Israel and brought judgment upon the people of God.

Christian-Muslim cooperation on overseas aid, relief and development

Natural disasters such as famines, earthquakes and tsunamis afflict entire populations, regardless of their faith. Relieving needs in such situations might seem an ideal way for Christians to show their love by cooperating with and funding Muslim-run initiatives. However, it must be recalled that when Muslims give their *zakat* offerings these are to be used for the benefit of their fellow-Muslims. (See page 23.) In accordance with this theology, Muslim aid agencies do not usually help all disaster victims irrespective of faith. The norm is that Muslim agencies only help Muslims. After the tsunami of December 26, 2004, many Christians in the strongly Islamic Indonesian province of Aceh found that they were refused aid unless they agreed to convert to Islam. This is by no means unusual.

It can be very hard for Christians to grasp this mindset, which is so deeply embedded in the Muslim psyche that it is often not verbalized, but simply taken for granted. In Islam there is simply no concept of loving outside the *umma* or of loving one's enemy. (Equally, it can be very hard for Muslims to understand that Christians may delight in giving aid to those of other faiths, with no strings attached – a policy which therefore often raises Muslim suspicions.) It is also important to realize that even though a Muslim aid agency may say on its website that it helps people of all faiths, this is highly unlikely to be what really happens on the ground. Certainly, Christian minorities in Muslim-majority contexts do not expect to receive help from Islamic sources. Even government aid might be denied them if local officials in charge of distribution decide not to give it to Christian villages or Christian families.

Another factor which applies to some Muslim aid agencies is the close link in the Muslim mind between helping Muslim needy and supporting the general Muslim cause. This means that donations made for "the poor" could possibly end up being used to fund *da'wa* or even *jihad*.

If Christians choose to make donations to Muslim aid agencies or to become associated with Muslim aid agencies, they must be aware that they are endorsing at the very least discrimination against their Christian brothers and sisters, and possibly activities which are far more anti- Christian than that. When Christian Aid donated £250,000 to Islamic Relief to assist the victims of the Pakistan earthquake of October 2005, did they consider that those who had specifically chosen a Christian agency through which to make their donation might not have wanted their gifts to be channeled through a Muslim agency?

In June 2007, the US-based United Methodist Committee on Relief (UMCOR), the relief arm of the United Methodist Church, announced a new partnership with the UK-based Muslim Aid which could result in $15 million in direct relief to areas such as Sri Lanka and Indonesia. The general secretary of Global Ministries, the parent organization of UMCOR, described how his organization worked alongside Muslim Aid in a mainly Muslim town in Sri Lanka, which led to this "new ground-breaking partnership."[94] It was unclear what attention would be given to Christian minorities in Sri Lanka or Indonesia, but according to UMCOR's general secretary the partnership intends to be a new model of working "together to help humanity."

When a senior evangelical bishop in the Church of England visited Afghanistan with an Islamic aid agency, what message did that send in a country where Christians are severely persecuted and converts from Islam have been killed? When another bishop in the Church of England visited Aceh, Indonesia, with Muslim Aid in July 2005 and cut the ribbon at the opening ceremony of the first new house for tsunami victims to be completed with funds from Muslim Aid, what message did that send to the beleaguered Acehnese Christians? Many Muslim Acehnese had already made it clear that they wanted to take advantage of the post-tsunami chaos to cleanse their province of Christians. The English bishop, who has a leading role in Christian-Muslim relations in the UK, was aware that there were non-Muslims in Aceh affected by the tsunami but apparently he made no effort to meet them, assist them, or affirm them in any way.[95] It is understandable that he was thrilled with the "immense privilege" of speaking at the opening ceremony of the Muslim Aid house, and "deeply moved" to be invited to cut the ribbon "hand in hand with a Muslim friend".

But it is very hard to comprehend his attitude if indeed he did not show any concern for the welfare of his Christian brothers and sisters in Indonesia, nor take time to find out how they were faring.

It is interesting to note that the group of British Muslims and Christians visiting Aceh to look at relief work after the tsunami was sponsored by the UK's Foreign Office. This is an example of how Western governments may be involved in driving forward the interfaith agenda.

Christian-Muslim cooperation on religious projects

As we have seen, in these days of rampant secularism some Christians are beginning to feel that they have a bond with people of any faith, as religious believers stand together against atheism, materialism, immorality and other features of secular society. This is possibly why some Western Christians have been willing to entertain suggestions such as that made by an imam in Woking, UK that a 2007 calendar be produced with texts from both the Bible and the Qur'an to be given to all Muslims and Christians in Woking. The local Christian cross-cultural ministry, whose aim is to "reach the nations in Woking," thought this might be "a great way to spread the Word." One wonders if they had considered the implications. Would the calendar, for example, put sura 4, verse 171 (which denies the Sonship of Christ) next to John 3:16, as if "balancing out" the truth claims? How far should Christians be involved in promoting the Qur'an, a book which denies Christ's death and resurrection (see page 55). Such a project could run the severe risk of sending the message to Christians that the Bible and Qur'an are equally valid as the Word of God.

Evangelicals at the Washington DC-based International Center for Religion and Diplomacy (ICRD) have, since 2003, been working together with Pakistani religious and civic organizations in "helping teachers of Pakistan's madrasas (Islamic religious schools) to provide a better education and improved moral guidance for their students by conducting teacher-training workshops."[96] These *madrassas* are notorious breeding grounds of Islamic radicals and generally provide little education apart from the Qur'an. ICRD is using government and private funding in seeking to promote peace and tolerance through *madrassa* reform, partnering with two prominent Islamic leaders from Pakistan, one a Wahhabi and the other a Deobandi. (Although not as extreme as Wahhabis, Deobandis are also a radical branch of Sunni Islam. They reject all Western influence and seek to return to classical Islam.)

ICRD Director Douglas M. Johnston believes that success "has been a function of (1) conducting the project in such a way that the madrasas feel it is their own reform effort and not something imposed from the outside (by giving them significant ownership in the process) and (2) inspiring them with their own heritage, pointing out how many of the pioneering breakthroughs in the arts and sciences, including religious tolerance, took place under Islam a thousand years ago."[97] According to a March 2008 news report, nearly 15,000 *madrassas* had registered with Pakistan's Ministry of Religious Affairs in the previous year, pledging "not to teach or promote militancy or religious hatred."[98] What changes in curriculum are occurring is not readily available, but if ICRD's main partners in Pakistan are a Wahhabi and a Deobandi, what is likely to be the nature of the "reform" introduced at the *madrassas*?

This illustrates the difficulty facing Christians who cooperate with Muslims in religious projects: how can they be sure they are cooperating with moderates working for moderation and modernity, rather than with conservatives such as Wahhabis and Deobandis, who will aim to establish extremism?

These kind of interfaith efforts, in the form of public-private efforts, have increased rapidly in the United States since September

11. The Middle East Initiative, sponsored by the US State Department and members of Congress, is another such effort, intended to "combine economics and faith."[99] The director of the faith component, former Democratic congressman Tony Hall, described the initiative's purpose in "connect(ing) people who are interested in peace and who come from the three major religions: Jews, Christians, and Muslims."[100] Hall continues, "We've tried diplomacy; we've tried might. Why don't we try asking God what he thinks and try to work through people of faith?" Why would this work, one might ask? Because, Hall explains, asserting a well-intentioned but unsubstantiated[101] pillar for interfaith understanding, "One major commandment of the three religions is to love our neighbors as we love ourselves."

Increasingly the US and other Western governments are concerned about the growing extremism within the Islamic world and the accompanying terrorist acts emanating from that religion. They have thus created a policy of engagement and have increasingly used Christian organizations and church leaders to pursue this agenda. The danger for the Church is that, in allowing itself effectively to become an arm of government, it will become lost in an interfaith morass and tie itself to government policies, thereby discrediting itself. Furthermore, it sends the message to the Muslim world that Christianity is indeed an arm of the State, as Muslims tend to believe anyway. It also sends the message to Christians in the Muslim world, who are often deeply conservative in their theology and faith, that the Church in the West is willing to sacrifice its beliefs in order to promote government policies.

In the United States this tendency has had negative effects on the mission and evangelism programs of two prominent theological seminaries. In an article about Fuller Theological Seminary, *The Los Angeles Times* announced that:

One of the nation's leading evangelical seminaries has launched a federally
funded project for making peace with Muslims, featuring a proposed code
of ethics that rejects offensive statements about each other's faiths, affirms
a mutual belief in one God and pledges not to proselytize.[102]

It was, said the reporter, "the latest of several efforts that Fuller has
launched since September 11 to build bridges with Muslims."

The seminary sought to address concerns and answer questions
it received in the aftermath of the news story via an informational
webpage[103] introduced by its Director of Public Relations. After
describing its faculty's "specific expertise in conflict resolution and
also in intercultural ministry and education," it addressed concern
over the prohibition against evangelism:

> The goal of this project is not to proselytize. It was felt that the goal of really
> understanding each other – Christians and Muslims – would be hindered if
> either group had an additional focus. But our work on this two-year project
> is only one part of our overall Islamic studies efforts, and in no way rules out
> or lessens our commitment to evangelism in other efforts.

Fuller President, Dr. Richard Mouw explained how "this is an
especially important time for us to be working for the common
good with our Muslim neighbors, especially in encouraging those
strands of Muslim thought that place a strong emphasis on the
peace-making passages in the Koran."

In a section titled "Do Muslims and Christians worship the same
God," he states,

> [T]he fact is that Christianity, Judaism and Islam trace their respective
> faiths back to Abraham. We need to explore with Muslims where
> we start to diverge in our understanding of the faith that Abraham
> nurtured. Muslims' faith in the God of Abraham gives us a common
> foundation upon which we can talk with them about the need for the
> sovereign grace that can only reach into our lives through the shed
> blood of Calvary.

However, under the rules of the project, as described in *The Los Angeles Times*, speaking about such matters would no doubt be forbidden. The reporter notes, "Muslim leaders, who regard tensions with evangelical Christians as one of their greatest interfaith challenges, say they are delighted by the Fuller initiative."

For Hartford Seminary in Connecticut, the rot set in much earlier. Hartford, one of America's oldest theological schools, was founded in 1834 by Calvinists who left Yale College to start a new institution of Christian learning. In the early decades of the twentieth century Hartford was a leading institution in the evangelization of Muslims. Samuel M. Zwemer (1867-1952), the famous missionary to Muslims, wrote:

> We hope to point out … the true solution to the Moslem problem, namely the evangelization of Moslems and to awaken sympathy, love and prayer on behalf of the Moslem world until its bonds are burst, its wounds are healed, its sorrows removed and its desires satisfied in Jesus Christ.

In 1911, Zwemer founded an academic quarterly titled *The Moslem World*, which offered information on Islam and was a forum for Christian mission strategy among Muslims. He served as its editor for 36 years, and then handed the responsibilities of running it over to others at Hartford Seminary on the condition that they remain in the same spirit of evangelism and commitment to evangelical truth.

One of the lecturers at Hartford at the turn of the twentieth century was the Scotsman, Duncan Black Macdonald (1863-1943), who taught Arabic and Islam. A highly respected scholar of Islam, Macdonald held that the seminary students must learn the language and theological heritage of Islam if they were to be successful in evangelizing Muslims. Macdonald's principles, controversial in his own time, later became an important part of Hartford's missionary training. However, the results may not have been what he anticipated, because, in the words of the current Hartford president, Heidi Hadsell, "The missionaries that we sent were coming home saying [Muslims] already believe in God. What we need is dialogue between Muslims and Christians."

Thirty years after Macdonald's death, in 1973, Hartford created the Duncan Black Macdonald Center for the Study of Islam and Christian-Muslim Relations. Its mission is to nurture Christian-Muslim understanding. In 1998, the center hired Ingrid Mattson, a Canadian-born convert to Islam with a doctorate in Islamic studies from the University of Chicago, to direct the chaplaincy program. Mattson is also the first female president of the Islamic Society of North America. In 2000 an Islamic chaplaincy program was launched at Hartford to train Muslims to be chaplains in any kind of institution – military, medical or prison. The number of students taking the Islamic chaplaincy training has steadily increased since then.

Today, Muslims make up 35 percent of the student body at Hartford Seminary, an institution which a few generations ago was training Christians to evangelize Muslims.

The case of Hartford Seminary shows how the laudable desire to understand Islam and Muslims has brought a seminary with a strong missionary emphasis to the point of using its resources to train and equip Muslims to strengthen other Muslims in their faith.

Reconciliation

Many current Christian initiatives towards Muslims describe their aim as "reconciliation" though it is unclear what the biblical justification for this choice of terminology is. Space does not permit a detailed study of the concept of reconciliation in the Bible, but the key passage often quoted in the context of Christian-Muslim relations, that is, the "ministry of reconciliation" (2 Corinthians 5:18-20), is clearly defined as reconciliation between sinful humans and God, not reconciliation between people of different faiths. Similarly most of the other New Testament references to reconciliation are defined within the text as reconciliation to God (Romans 5:10; 11:15; Ephesians 2:16; Colossians 1:20,22). The only exceptions are reconciliation between estranged spouses (1 Corinthians 7:11) and between fellow believers who have quarreled (Matthew 5:24). As for the Old Testament, the whole tenor is against any kind of rapprochement between the people of God and followers of another faith. The word reconciliation is used in some translations in the context of atonement for sin i.e. reconciliation of sinners with God. The one exception occurs in 1 Samuel 29:4 where the Philistines anticipate that David may seek to be reconciled to Saul and thus turn traitor to them.

While we are called to love all human beings regardless of creed, race or culture, there is no call in the Bible for Christians as a body to seek reconciliation with other faiths. (Rather, such action would stand in danger of judgment, at least according to the Old Testament.) This is not to deny the need for Christians and Muslims to find ways of addressing the causes of contemporary conflict with a view to sharing the globe harmoniously. In this area of conflict it is vital for Christians to be peacemakers (Matthew 5:9). But peace should never be made at the expense of theological distinctives or at the expense of righteousness, justice and truth.

Hans Küng has argued "No peace among the nations without peace between the religions." The difficulty with this argument is that it presupposes a level playing field. Whereas Christianity (bar some aspects of Orthodox denominations) has abandoned religious territoriality, Islam has not. Therefore to argue for peace without a profound change in Islamic understanding of territory is not viable.

There are also Christians who propound the need for reconciliation in the context of specific perceived historical injustices perpetrated by Christians on Muslims e.g. the Crusades and colonialism. The methodology is usually to apologize for what European or other

Western Christians are deemed to have done. The Yale Center's Christian response to the Muslim clerics' letter does exactly this, "acknowledging that in the past (e.g. in the Crusades) and in the present (e.g. in excesses of the 'war on terror') many Christians have been guilty of sinning against our Muslim neighbors."[104]

The motivation is usually either to prepare the way for the effective evangelization of Muslims by seeking their forgiveness or simply to facilitate harmonious Christian-Muslim relations. Some also believe that such apologies will cleanse the land where blood has been spilled and so usher in God's blessings. Sadly such positions are based on weak theology and inaccurate historical understanding.

This is not to suggest that Christians have never failed and that there are never times when apology is appropriate. But apologizing for the Crusades and for colonialism sends inappropriate cultural signals and can do more harm than good in that they reinforce the Muslims' sense of grievance against Christians. In the case of the Yale Center statement, the "acknowledgement" became the focal point in much of the Muslim world's reporting on the release of public letter.[105] The tragic result is often a backlash of Muslim violence against vulnerable Christian minorities in the Muslim countries. Reconciliation has no value if it is devoid of righteousness, justice and truth.

There is no theology of reconciliation in the *shari'a*, only a theology of temporary treaties. Permanent peace can only exist within *Dar al-Islam*, i.e. where Muslims are in control. A further complication is that reconciliation is one of the situations in which Muslims are specifically permitted to lie, according to the doctrine of *taqiyya* (see page 38).

Mission and evangelism

Christian spirituality cannot remove mission from its core. It has been said that the Church is mission - a mission-less Church is a Christ-less Church. The Church's encounter with Islam must carry a missionary dimension. This dimension will involve a loving, compassionate service and witness that confidently proclaims the truths of the Gospel, trusting God for the result.

Mission to Muslims will be rooted in prayer and intercession and will challenge the spiritual principalities and powers that make up Islam. It will deal with power encounters as did the Lord Jesus in his ministry.

None of the above cautions about Christian-Muslim relations should prevent Western Christians from seeking to make friends with Muslims, to show Muslims love and compassion, to share their faith with Muslims, or to invite Muslims to church as members of the congregation (as opposed to inviting Muslims to preach or lead prayer or worship in a church service).

As there are many works devoted to advising Christians on the practicalities of sharing their faith with Muslims, this subject will not be covered in detail here.[106] Much help in missionary methods can also be found by drawing on the experience of missionaries working amongst Muslims in the Muslim world and in the West, and also on the expertise of Christians from the Muslim world living in the West. One caution to note is that missionary methods which depend on contextualization must be used with great care. For they run the risk of contextualizing not just culture but theology as well. This can be strongly counter-productive, in that Christian mission can inadvertently become part of Islamic *da'wa*. It can also create numerous problems for the converts.

Ultimately, it is not our method that is important but our attitude, which should be born out of love. We should have lives filled with the Holy Spirit. We should have faith in God that he will do the work of conversion.

In terms of "how," perhaps there is no better pattern for us to follow than that of the Lord Jesus himself, who was love incarnate. The way he dealt with others can be our model in dealing with Muslims. Our lives, as his disciples, should portray his beauty and his loveliness as we minister to Muslims.

1. As Jesus came and **lived among us**, so his disciples today are incarnated within many different contexts. In situations of danger, hardship, poverty and disaster, Christ's followers are present.

2. As Jesus **went about doing good**, as he came not to be served but to serve, so his followers are at work within their communities, holding forth the love of Christ through their service to others.

3. Like Jesus, his followers **teach and preach** the good news to those who do not understand, to those who have misunderstood the nature of the Christian faith. This will involve the defense of the doctrines of the Christian faith with Muslims attack, for example, the deity and death of Christ, the reliability of the Bible, as well as explaining aspects of the Christian faith which are misunderstood in Islam, such as the Sonship of Christ and the Trinity.

4. As Christ **engaged the powers of darkness**, for he saw that the world is in the hands of the Evil One, so his followers engage in spiritual warfare. They realize that their struggle is not against flesh and blood but against the spiritual forces of evil in the heavenly realms (Ephesians 6:12). Prayer is vital.

5. As Christ healed the sick and demonstrated God's power at work in human lives through **signs and wonders**, so his Spirit works through his disciples today in miraculous ways to bring healing and wholeness, visions and dreams.

6. As Christ **suffered** for his people on the cross, as he bled and died for them, so in a different way his people witness through their suffering. The Greek word for "witness" is *martus*, from

which the English "martyr" is derived, one who bears witness by his or her death. Tertullian's famous comment about the blood of the martyrs being the seed of the church has been proved true time and again in the 1800 years since.

7. As the Lord Jesus **loved his own** who were in the world, so their love for each other is a witness to him (John 13:1,34,35). He commanded them, "As I have loved you, so you must love one another," and told them what would happen if they did. "By this all men will know that you are my disciples, if you love one another."

One vital element of effective evangelism is that Christians should be well taught about the differences between Islam and Christianity. In this way they will be equipped to resist the approaches of Muslims seeking to convert them to Islam, and will have a balanced understanding of the whole of Islamic doctrine and practice. This is necessary because what is presented in the secular media and by Muslims themselves on the nature of Islam is often only partial and sometimes even misleading. Teaching should address the confusion which currently exists concerning the inter-relationship of Islam and Christianity and will especially address the popular concept of Islam and Christianity sharing the same beliefs and moral values in contradistinction to the secular world.

An aspect of growing concern amongst Christians is how to understand the End Times in relation to Islam. Some, for example, have equated Islam with the antichrist of John's epistles. It is worth noting that the second coming of Jesus figures highly in Islamic eschatology together with the beast, the antichrist and Armageddon. (See page 22.) Although Islam is clear about its own position in the End Times, it is difficult for Christians to be so sure because it is not clearly delineated in the Bible. It is much more important for those who us to be assured that Jesus is coming again, that he will rule victoriously over heaven and earth, that the gates of hell will not prevail against his Church and that Satan will be defeated.

Convert care

This important subject should perhaps not come under the heading of Christian-Muslim relations because it is really Christian-Christian relations. However, it is placed here to emphasize that it should be an integral part of mission to Muslims.

Compared with new believers from a secular or nominally Christian background, the needs of converts from Islam are usually far greater. This is true of practical, emotional and spiritual needs. The challenge to churches is to care for the converts and meet these needs. Many Muslim converts who have not been cared for well enough eventually choose to return to Islam, a faith which excels at caring for its own.

Apostasy law in Islam

Conversion from Islam is viewed as treachery against the Muslim community and this is the basis for the extreme reaction of Muslim friends, family, colleagues etc. When Islamic law lays down the death sentence for adult male apostates from Islam it is executing them as if they were traitors. While the death sentence for apostasy is only part of the law of the land in a handful of countries (e.g. Saudi Arabia, Iran, Sudan, Mauritania) it cannot be emphasized too much that the apostasy law is acknowledged by the vast majority of Muslims to be part of their theology. Hence the persecution of converts from Islam by a multiplicity of methods of attacking the person, their property, relationships and freedoms. This can even include murder, to which some Muslim police officers would turn a blind eye.

A British imam seeking to promote interfaith relations has proposed a scheme whereby Muslims may be permitted to convert to certain Christian denominations (i.e. not be persecuted for doing so). He proposes that agreements could be made between Muslim authorities and the Orthodox and Roman Catholic churches. The denominational leaders would have to pledge their solidarity with various international Muslim causes (Palestine, Iraq etc.) and condemn US foreign policy. On these conditions, the Muslims would agree not to persecute any Muslims who converted to these particular denominations. The imam envisages that Anglicans – being such a broad church – would most likely have to be dealt with in two groups. He anticipates that it would probably be possible to make an agreement with Anglo-Catholics but not with evangelical Anglicans. He doubts that converts to other Protestant denominations would be eligible for such agreements. (Separately he requires restrictions on foreign missionaries evangelizing in Muslim countries.)

Such an initiative should not be countenanced by Christians, as it makes the Church submit to the requirements of Islam and effectively enshrines the continued persecution of converts to conservative evangelical Christianity, divides the Church, and forces Christians to abandon the Great Commission without making any such requirement for Muslims to stop engaging in *da'wa*. This is contrary to Article 18 of the United Nations Universal Declaration of Human Rights which guarantees the freedom to change one's religion or belief.

What converts suffer

The "crime" of apostasy brings enormous shame on the relatives of the convert, and therefore the relatives will go to any lengths to try to persuade the convert to return to Islam and thus restore the family's honor. Often baptism is the point at which severe persecution begins.

A typical reaction will be threats and perhaps violence from some family members, or emotional blackmail such as a distraught mother saying she will kill herself if her beloved child does not return to Islam. Bearing in mind that the closest bond in many Muslim families is between mother and son, this can be extremely hard for a young man to bear. Another kind of threat or pressure is financial, for example, refusing to assist a convert student with their fees or support. A married convert may find that the spouse leaves, taking the children too. Many converts have to leave home – either they are thrown out or they have to escape the pressure and violence. There can also be rejection and violence from the wider Muslim community, for example, stoning, arson, beatings – all these have been experienced by converts from Islam living in the UK.

So the local church **must** become the convert's new family. Their "family responsibilities" must be as wide- ranging and deep in commitment as a Muslim family's are (Muslim families tend to be more supportive than a typical Western family). That includes providing accommodation, friendship, fellowship and financial support if necessary. The emotional pain of rejection by family and friends is something which cannot quickly be healed, but the continued patient love of Christians plays an essential part.

In Muslim countries it can be very risky for Christians who care for converts from Islam and sadly some churches will therefore not get involved. But in the West there is nothing to stop churches taking responsibility for caring for such converts. The fact that some British church leaders have publicly refused to accept Muslim converts amounts to disobedience to Jesus' command to his disciples to love one another. The motive appears to be a fear of jeopardizing harmonious Christian-Muslim relations locally.

Relations between Christians and the Muslim community are important, but the needs of converts from Islam – Christians who are carrying a heavy cross – must take precedence. It is grotesque and nonsensical to neglect the needs of Christian converts from

Islam for the sake for friendship with Muslims; we must not sacrifice the members of our own family on the altar of our post-modern relativism.

New Christians from a Muslim background often feel in great need of spiritual guidance. They have left a faith which is characterized by a multitude of rules governing even which foot to step over a threshold with, how to lie in bed, and how to relieve oneself.[107] Their new faith does not have this framework of rules, so converts can feel unsure how to behave in many situations. They need discipleship training to help them learn to live and grow as Christians.

Asylum-seekers

Many British churches may have links with converts from Islam who are not British citizens and do not have "indefinite leave to remain" in the UK. Such individuals could be sent back to their country of origin, which in turn could endanger their lives because of Islam's apostasy laws and the effect this has on Muslim society. The same situation can arise in other Western countries but appears to be particularly acute in the UK, where many immigration officers do not yet seem to understand or believe the real dangers which converts face. They often fail to distinguish between Christian-background Christians and Muslim-background Christians, and do not recognize that the former may be safe while the latter are at risk. They also often seem to be unaware that what the law or constitution of the country says about guaranteeing freedom of religion may be contradicted by what happens in practice on the ground.

Converts who do not have a good command of English face the additional risk of possibly having a Muslim interpreter who may not do justice to what they are saying, or who may report them to the local Muslim community, thus placing them in further danger.

Churches must exert themselves to assist such individuals or families in their legal battles. Finding a lawyer experienced in such cases is vital.

Involvement in society

Islam, alone among world faiths, has very clear-cut aims for reorganizing society to conform to its teaching. Because of this, Muslim minorities are impacting their host societies in the West in a way which no other faith is doing. Christians with a concern for their society and who recognize that Islam is more than just personal belief are active in seeking to alert decision-makers at national and local level to the implications of changes which are being made to accommodate the Muslim community in such areas as law, finance and education. This increasingly involves both social and political action.

Justice

Christians in the West have the freedom to speak out and lobby on any issue they like. There is therefore a challenge for the Church in terms of making use of this freedom to be a voice for persecuted Christians in Muslim contexts who cannot speak for themselves. The Bible teaches clearly that God loves justice, and Western Christians are in a position to work for justice for their fellow-Christians who suffer discrimination and oppression for no other reason than their Christian faith.

Key issues are the apostasy law and *dhimmi* status as enshrined in the *shari'a*, which includes discrimination against Christians in terms of legal testimony and compensation. (See page 73.) The theology of *jihad* lies behind some anti-Christian violence, such as that which various provinces of Indonesia have seen in the early years of the twenty-first century. Another important issue is that of "blasphemy" against Muhammad, who is so venerated in Pakistan that, as we have seen, there is a mandatory death sentence for "defiling" his name. As has already been noted, Christians are particularly vulnerable to malicious accusations under this law, because of the tendency of some Muslim judges to believe the word of a Muslim over that of a Christian (in accordance with *shari'a*).

Another kind of injustice faced repeatedly by Christian minorities in the Muslim world is the way in which they are made scapegoats for the actions of governments and others in "Christian" countries of the West. Thus in January and February 2006 Christians in Iraq, Nigeria, Turkey and Pakistan and many other countries faced threats or actual violence in response to the publication in a number of secular newspapers in Europe of caricatures of Muhammad which had originally been drawn by Danish cartoonists in 2005. Even Christian children were victimized for the actions of the European journalists when church schools in Pakistan were attacked. As the Bishop of Peshawar said, "We [Pakistani Christians] have not done anything; the cartoons are nothing to do with us. They [the Muslim rioters] do not comprehend or accept that Pakistani Christians are not Westerners."

Furthermore, Christian minorities have to accept the desecration of what is sacred to them without being able to complain. The Pakistani rioters at Mardan on February 6, 2006 were reported to have made a large cross, then trampled on it and burned it. They were retaliating for what they held to be an insult to their prophet (as were hundreds of thousands of other Muslims around the world) in the full knowledge that the Christian minority in Pakistan could do nothing about it.

It is possible that the freedom to protest against such injustice may not continue in the West indefinitely. Victoria State, Australia, already has its Racial and Religious Tolerance Act (2001), which has been used to prevent Christians from teaching other Christians about Islam. The UK narrowly escaped similar legislation being passed in January 2006, which could well have stopped any criticism of Islam or its treatment of non-Muslim minorities. Christians must take up this challenge while they still can.

The issue of justice for Christian minorities is one which – like the issue of converts from Islam – can easily become sidelined in the desire for "dialogue" and good Christian-Muslim relations. But this amounts to a betrayal of vulnerable Christians. In January 2006 Dr Mouneer Hanna Anis, the Anglican Bishop in Egypt, met with senior Egyptian Muslim clerics at Trinity College, Dublin to launch a resource pack called "The Hand of History (Exploring Christian/Muslim Dialogue)." One of the Muslims was the Grand Mufti of Egypt and Rector of the prestigious Al-Azhar University in Cairo, the leading institution of Sunni Islam worldwide. The other Muslim was Al-Azhar's president of the Dialogue with Monotheistic Religions.

The bishop made several statements about the situation of Egyptian Christians to the effect that those of Christian background had virtually no problems and even converts from Islam had only minor difficulties. Such statements cannot be described as anything less than extremely misleading (not to say painful to those whose sufferings were being denied), and dialoguing in rose-tinted spectacles seems at best pointless. One wonders whether the bishop realized how his statements could be quoted by others to the detriment of the very needy and vulnerable Christians of Egypt. The Metropolitan of Glastonbury, who heads the British Orthodox Church which is an integral part of the Coptic Orthodox Church, wrote to the Archbishop of Canterbury, criticizing Dr Mouneer's assertions, pointing out the grave difficulties facing Egyptian Christians, and finishing:

Brotherly support from the Anglican community worldwide, and especially in Egypt is something much to be valued, but if it is to be of lasting value in enabling the diverse religious communities to live together in harmony, it is also necessary to highlight the source and reality of the problems which militate against this. [108]

Conclusion

This book has sought to demonstrate that Islam is an all-encompassing entity which includes not only the inner life but also, and especially, the outer life of an individual's role in family, community and society. Neither law nor politics nor military service lies outside of Islam. It has also sought to show the rigid, highly specified and unchanging nature of Islam which leaves little or no freedom for the individual's conscience or personality to be expressed, or for Islam itself to alter or adapt. That the contemporary Islamic renewal movement is seeking to impose the age-old Islamic societal norms wherever it can, even by force, should be no surprise as it is the very essence of Islam to take control of earthly structures.

The crisis which arose in early 2006 over the publication of cartoons of Muhammad the Islamic prophet well illustrated the way in which Islam operates. Islam has the capacity for thinking strategically, acting structurally and working towards submission of non-Muslims. This is done primarily through fear. The West is now at a crossroads in its relationship with Islam. Threats and intimidation have resulted in pusillanimous governments, compliant media and an insipid Church. The fear which is beginning to shape government and media has now sadly entered into the Church, with Christians increasingly unwilling or unable to critique Islam. Either they embrace dialogue and interfaith relations and acquiesce, in the name of tolerance, to

Muslim demands on the Muslims' terms or they retreat into a ghetto-like mentality born of fear. For the Christian we are told that perfect love casts out fear, for there can be no fear in love (1 John 4:18). Christians who truly love God and their Savior, the Lord Jesus Christ, will not fear what either people or ideology or false religion can do to them. The time has come for the Church to stand up and be bold in the face of an oncoming darkness. The Church needs great faith and courage to be strong in our day. She can do so with the conviction and assurance that it is the Lord who builds his Church and the gates of hell will not prevail against that Church. For a Church that is no longer convinced of truth needs to rediscover Jesus as the Truth, and should be willing, if need be, to die for that Truth, which is Jesus. If we do not have the courage to speak the truth in love and witness to our faith we shall be like the Church in the early days of Islam which succumbed and was eradicated.

In our day we can be thankful to God for the growing numbers of Muslims who are coming to Christ - more than ever before in history. Yet we must also be aware of the success of the many Islamic *da'wa* initiatives, whether through formal agencies or informally, who are converting Westerners to Islam, sometimes even committed Christians. One of the most effective of these methods is that of Muslim men marrying Western women. As Christians become less certain of their faith, as the concept of Islam and Christianity as sibling "Abrahamic" faiths gains ground, many Christian women do not seem to see any theological objection to marrying a Muslim, and very often they go on to embrace his faith for themselves.[109] We must also recognize the advance of *da'wa* initiatives at a societal and structural level. As Muslims in the West develop an Islamic consciousness and visiblity, set up their own institutions, and work for political recognition of their faith community, these are but stages along the route of Islamizing the whole of their host society –

at least in the minds of some Muslims. There are those who would even be prepared to use violence if necessary to achieve the final stage of creating an Islamic state.

The most devout and sincere Muslims include those who are most active in seeking political power. Concern for the welfare of Muslims should not diminish our concern for the countries in which we live. Where the Judeo-Christian ethic is the basis of society, this should not be abandoned or diluted, but rather affirmed. The revival of political Islam in the last few decades means that a re-evaluation of the present crisis in Christian-Muslim relations is necessary. It is not wise to continue harking back to the memory of the "good old days" that occurred under colonialism and before the rise of radical Islam, which on closer inspection may not have been so harmonious anyway.

Although superficially similar, Islam and Christianity are very far from being sibling religions. Not only does Islam specifically deny a series of key theological beliefs and creedal statements of Christianity, but also the whole basis of the faith is different. Christianity emphasizes the premise that God is love. "Only from the perspective of God's all-surpassing love revealed in Christ can man finally acknowledge that love is the meaning of reality (cf. John 3:16; Romans 5:6-11)."[110] Duty and works cannot save us. In Islam duty and works are the way to heaven although Muslims can never be sure of their eternal destiny.

If "love is the meaning of reality" for Christians, then power is the meaning of reality for Muslims. Power and its accompanying prestige must be gained at all costs. There is no place in Islam for a suffering God, and human vulnerability is likewise spurned. But the glory of Christianity is the vulnerability and human suffering born out of our understanding of the suffering of God in Christ Jesus. To the Muslim mind this is an appalling thought.

In the Gospel we encounter God in Christ who reconciles the world to himself. The suffering Christ is none other than the redeemer of the world. To share him means to witness to his redemptive and vicarious death, even to our Muslim friends and neighbors. We are called to rediscover what Paul means in sharing the whole counsel of God with tears and trembling. The love of Christ must renew and move the Church afresh to see him more clearly, love him more dearly, follow him more nearly and confess him more boldly in our day and age. This is the road to recover a new confidence in the Gospel.

Christian spirituality is founded on a suffering God who sent his only Son to earth, taking the form of a servant and sacrificing himself for humankind. The vulnerability and powerlessness that characterize the Christian faith must also define the relationship of Christians to Muslims. There can be no hate, bigotry or fear. The Christian modeled after his or her Master will seek the salvation of Muslims, in the words of Raymond Lull, "by love, by tears and by self-giving." In conclusion, as we explore relations between Muslims and Christians it is vital that we seek scholarly accuracy, that our hearts are filled with compassionate concern for Muslims as human beings, and that we remain utterly faithful to Christ and to his revelation.

Appendix

Barnabas Fund Response to the Yale Center for Faith and Culture Statement ("Loving God and Neighbor Together"...)

January 24, 2008

History

The Pope's Regensburg lecture. On September 12, 2006, Pope Benedict XVI gave a lecture on faith and reason at Regensburg University, Germany.[1] Muslims around the world were offended by one passage, taken out of its context, in which he quoted a Byzantine Emperor on Islam and violence. Angry and violent demonstrations by Muslims erupted around the world. Christians in Muslim lands bore the brunt of the violence: churches were damaged and several Christians killed. Many Muslim leaders, including the influential International Union for Muslim Scholars (IUMS), demanded an apology from the Pope.

Letter to Pope from 38 Muslim scholars. In October 2006, 38 Muslim scholars wrote a letter to Pope Benedict XVI, correcting what they perceived as several errors in his presentation of Islam in the Regensburg address. One interesting statement they made was that the Qur'anic verse "There is no compulsion in religion . . ." (Q2:256) was

---

1 Full text of the Pope's lecture can be found at: http://chiesa.espresso.republica.it/articolo/83303?&eng=y

revealed during Muhammad's Medinan period when he was in a position of strength. They thus implied, but did not categorically state, that it was not abrogated by other later verses (the traditional majority opinion). The Vatican did not write an answer to the letter, but stated that the Pope had been misunderstood by Muslims, and that the intent of his speech had been a call for cooperation and dialogue with Muslims.[2]

Tim Winter, a British convert to Islam (also known as Abdul Hakim Murad) who is Sheikh Zayed lecturer in Islamic studies at the Divinity School, University of Cambridge, explained that the letter was an attempt by Muslim leaders to address misunderstandings of Islam current in the West, caused by the rise of a violent fringe in Islam. It appears that Muslim leaders feel that they are failing to communicate effectively with Christians in the West, partly because Islam lacks a centralized point of authority to speak on their behalf in the way that they consider the Vatican and the Pope speak on behalf of Christians. It would seem that these scholars, representing over 20 countries and 8 different streams of Islam, and brought together by the Aal al-Bayt Institute for Islamic Thought in Amman, Jordan, were trying to establish themselves as a cross-denominational Islamic authority – certainly an innovation in Islam.

"A Common Word", letter to Christian leaders from 138 Muslim scholars. On October 13, 2007, 138 Muslim scholars wrote an open letter, "A Common Word Between Us and You", addressed to world Christian leaders. It was organized by the Royal Aal al-Bayt Institute for Islamic Thought in Jordan, which is supported by the Jordanian Royal House and the Royal Academy in Jordan. This organization seeks to solidify an international, interdenominational body of Muslim religious scholars to represent the interests of Islam to governments, other religions and international bodies. Its Chairman of the Board of Trustees is Prince Ghazi bin Muhammad bin Talal of the Jordanian royal family. Its aim is to be seen as speaking on

2   Dan Murphy, "Muslim scholars write the pope – and everyone else", *Christian Science Monitor*, October 19, 2006; For the full text of the letter see: "Open Letter to His Holiness Pope Benedict XVI", http://www.islamicamagazine.com/media/pdf/open/b/openletter-8238DA.pdf viewed January 14, 2008.

behalf of all Muslims and setting policies and doctrines for all of Islam. At the same time it might be significant that Muslim-Brotherhood-affiliated scholars such as Yusuf al-Qaradawi, the most influential Sunni cleric in the Muslim world, and Tariq Ramadan (a very popular European-based Muslim scholar) were missing from the list of signatories in both letters. This might indicate some internal Muslim competition for the status of international representation of worldwide Islam.

Two obvious problems of the document are:

1. It totally ignores non-monotheistic religions such as Hinduism, Buddhism and others. This might imply that Islam's relationship to them is still the same as to the ancient polytheists who were given the choice of converting to Islam or being killed.

2. It almost completely ignores the Jewish people and Islam's attitude to them. This seems to fit with contemporary Muslim efforts to drive a wedge between Christians and Jews and form an alliance of Muslims and Christians against Jews who are increasingly bearing the brunt of a widespread Muslim anti-Semitic discourse.

The Yale Statement. On November 18, 2007, as a response to the October 2007 Muslim letter, some Evangelical Christian theologians at the Yale Center for Faith and Culture, Yale Divinity School, New Haven, Connecticut, published a letter which was then signed by over 100 Evangelical and other Christian theologians, pastors and ministry leaders. Formally entitled "Loving God and Neighbor Together: A Christian Response to 'A Common Word Between Us and You'", this letter is referred to as "The Yale Statement."[3] Dr. Miroslav Volf, Henry B. Wright Professor of Theology at Yale Divinity School and Director of the Center for Faith and Culture, received the thanks of Muslim scholars for his positive embrace of the Muslim initiative at a press conference held on November 26, 2007 at the Cultural Foundation of Abu Dhabi,

---

3 "Loving God And Neighbor Together: A Christian Response to 'A Common Word Between Us and You'", Yale Center for Faith and Culture, http://www.yale.edu/faith/abou-commonword.htm viewed January 11, 2008.

United Arab Emirates. The number of signatories rose to over 300 by mid-January 2008.

The signatories represent a wide spread of Christian leaders, including representatives of the National Association of Evangelicals (NAE) like Leith Anderson, its current president; representatives of the World Evangelical Alliance such as Geoff Tunnicliffe, International Director, and Bertil Ekstrom, Executive Director of its mission commission; and lecturers in religion, theology and Biblical studies at prestigious American universities such as Princeton, Yale, Hartford and Harvard, as well as at Evangelical seminaries such as Fuller Theological Seminary (including J. Dudley Woodberry, doyen of Evangelical Islamic studies and Dean Emeritus of Fuller).

The list also includes leaders of Evangelical mission societies and of Evangelical mission centers, including George Verwer and Peter Maiden of Operation Mobilization (OM); Lynn Green of Youth With a Mission (YWAM); the founder of Frontiers, Greg Livingstone (Frontiers are involved in contextualization of mission to Muslims); and Dwight P. Baker, Associate Director of Overseas Ministries Study Center (OMSC).

There are pastors of some of the largest Evangelical churches in the US, including Bill Hybels of Willow Creek and Rick Warren of Saddleback. There is a good sprinkling of Lutheran, Methodist, Presbyterian, Church of Christ, Assemblies of God, Mennonite and Baptist leaders. Several leading British Evangelicals also have signed the letter, including Christopher J H Wright, International Director of Langham Partnership International.

The list also includes Episcopal leaders in the US such as Bishop Barry Beisner of the Episcopal Diocese of Northern California and Peter J. Lee of Virginia; and a number of American Roman Catholic leaders and academics as well as a few Orthodox leaders.

Why did so many Christian leaders sign the Yale Statement? They surely all did it in good faith and with the best of intentions, but it is interesting to note the variety of motives which some have given when afterwards asked the reason that they signed:

1. Some believed it the right way to respond with Christian love and charity.

2. Some were motivated by fear of the potential for a global conflict with Islam, or specifically a conflict with Islam affecting the region in which they themselves live.

3. Some were hopeful that this response would open the way for a process of reconciliation between Islam and Christianity.

4. Some took a naively trusting approach, accepting the Muslim letter at face value without any suspicion of hidden agendas.

5. Some were particularly impressed by the wide spectrum of Muslim signatories and by the irenic tone of the letter, and saw it as a unique historical opportunity to mend fences with Islam.

6. Some took a pragmatic view that the developing dialogue could open the way for Christian missions and evangelism in Muslim lands and for freedom for Muslims to accept Christ and convert to Christianity.

7. Some did not study the document in detail but trusted the advice of others who encouraged them to sign.

Barnabas Fund analysis of "A Common Word." The Barnabas Fund published a response on November 28, 2007 in which the Muslim letter was closely analyzed. A further Barnabas Fund elucidation of the response, including insights from Christians living in the Muslim world, was published on January 7, 2008.[4] The Barnabas analysis saw the Muslim letter as falling into the tradition of Muslim *da'wa* (call to convert and submit to Islam) which was often linked historically to the threat of violent war and conquest (*jihad*), should the call be rejected. The Muslim letter clearly indicated the centrality of the concept of *tawhid* (the monolithic unity of God) and the finality of the prophethood of Muhammad as against the central Christian doctrines of the deity of

---

4   The Barnabas response can be found at http://www.barnabasfund.org/news/archives/article. php?ID_news_items=342

Christ and the Trinity. Jesus is reduced and Islamized to a mere human prophet subservient to Muhammad. Most of the Qur'an and *hadith* passages quoted included attacks on those who associate others with God – in traditional orthodox Islamic exegesis always interpreted as attacks on Christian "corruptions." Thus, what would superficially appear to be an offer of common ground in the love of God and one's neighbor, in reality turns out to be a missionary pamphlet extolling Islam and denigrating the very heart of Christianity. It seems likely that the Muslim authors assumed that Muslim readers would understand the veiled intentions while Christian readers not conversant with Muslim traditions would fail to understand.

138 Muslim scholars Christmas and New Year message: As a sign of gratitude for the generally positive Christian response, the Muslim scholars published "A Muslim Message of Thanks and of Christmas and New Year Greetings, December 2007," which among other places appeared as a full-page advertisement in *The Daily Telegraph*, December 29, 2007. In this message, the original *da'wa* themes of the letter were repeated, i.e. the centrality of the *tawhid* concept to Islam and the rebuke to Christians in the quotes mentioning "no associates."

The Vatican was rather slow to respond officially to the Muslim initiative. It seemed not so much interested in pure theological dialogue as in a more practical exchange that discussed the realities on the ground of Christians living in Muslim countries. Following a correspondence between the Vatican Secretary of State, Tarcisio Bertone, on behalf of the Pope, and the Jordanian Prince, Ghazi bin Muhammad bin Talal, clarifying the issues between the two sides, the way was opened for a summit meeting. The Pope stressed that he wanted to discuss respect for the dignity of all human beings, awareness of the other's religion, and a common commitment to promoting mutual tolerance among the younger generation. In other words, the Pope would not accept the limits set by the Muslim leaders of only discussing the theological implications of their statements on love of God and the neighbor, but wanted it expanded to include practical implementations in the Muslim world, including discussion of human rights and equality for non-Muslims. The Pope also stressed that the common ground between Muslims and Christians is their belief in One God who is creator and judge, rather than accept the Muslim letter's spurious definition of common ground between the two faiths as love for God and neighbor. The Jordanian prince insisted that the dialogue be limited to theological and spiritual themes. On January 2, 2008, Cardinal Jean-Louis Tauran, President of the Pontifical Council for Interreligious Dialogue, announced that a "historic" meeting will take place in spring 2008 between Pope Benedict XVI and a representative delegation of the 138 Muslim scholars, authors of the letter. The Muslim representatives will also meet with other Vatican institutions.[5]

The Rev. Christian W. Troll, a Jesuit scholar engaged in dialogue with Muslims, Honorary Professor at St. Georgen Graduate School of Theology and Philosophy, Frankfurt am Main, Germany, declared that there had never been an initiative like this letter in the 1,400 years of Muslim-Christian history. He welcomes the "warm, inviting tone" of the letter which is "enormously encouraging." He sees the Muslim call as a response to the Pope's Regensburg lecture which had the intent of provoking a deeper dialogue between Christianity and Islam. He notes the quotations from the Bible and wonders whether this signals a break with traditional Islamic doctrine and a new approach by Muslims to the Jewish and Christian scriptures. In other words, have the Muslim scholars repudiated the doctrine of the corruption of the Bible which is still the common Muslim view? Or, Troll asks, are they merely using selected Bible quotations to accentuate the Muslim views on God and love? Troll also notes that several of the Qur'anic quotations are used in

---

5   Sandro Magister, "The Cardinal Writes, the Prince Responds: The Factors that Divide the Pope from the Muslims", *Chiesa*, 2 January 2008, http://chiesa.espresso.repubblica.it/articolo/184641?eng=y viewed 11 January 2008.

traditional Muslim commentary as expressing criticism of the Christian doctrines on the divinity of Jesus. He warns that Muslims wanting to engage in dialogue with Christians must understand that the deity of Jesus and Trinitarian monotheism are basic doctrines that "cannot be negotiated away." Finally, Troll argues that in spite of any agreement on the "double-love commandment" there are still enormous problems in Muslim-Christian relations including the imposition of *shari'a*, the relationship between state and religion, and the deteriorating situation of many Christians living in Muslim majority countries.[6]

Samir Khalil Samir, a Jesuit Islamic scholar and lecturer at St Joseph University, Beirut. Samir approves of the greater convergence developing between various Islamic currents, evident in the signatories of the letter, which implies a concerted move towards a greater consensus (*ijma'*). He also welcomes their desire for dialogue with Christians, and sees this as a direct result of the Pope's "masterful" tactics. Samir notes that the Arabic text uses "Gospel" rather than Bible as in the English version. He further notes that the letter uses the Arabic word *jar* for neighbor (meaning a geographical proximity) rather than the Christian Arabic term *qarib* which includes the meaning of brother and is not dependent on geographical proximity. Samir explains that the word "love" is rarely used in the Qur'an, and what the Muslim scholars stress as love in the first part of the letter is actually obedience to God rather than love to Him. He says that while this talk of love for God and neighbor is a novelty in Islam, "it certainly shows a desire to draw near to the Christian way of speaking, even if at the same time there is the risk of taking two meanings from the same word." He points out that the declaration that Jews, Christians and Muslims have love of God and of one's neighbor at the heart of their respective faiths has never before been stated by Muslims. He also notes that when the Muslim scholars

---

6 Christian W. Troll, "Towards *common ground* between Christians and Muslims?" Posted on the Official Website of A Common Word, http://www.acommonword.com/index.php?page=responses&item=21 viewed January 15, 2008.

quote from the Qur'an they say "God said," while when quoting from the Bible they merely state "as is found in the New Testament" or "as is read in the Gospels." Samir presents the Catholic view that natural law is the real common ground between Christianity and other religions. He refutes the accusations against Christians as warring against Muslims, explaining that the issues concerning the war on terror are political issues: "Even if we know that the president of the United States is a Christian and that he is led by his faith, it can in no way be claimed that this is a war of Christians against Muslims." The Muslim stand is colored by their tendency to see the West as a Christian power, not accepting the reality of its secularization and estrangement from Christian ethics. Such Muslim presuppositions only reinforce the theory of a clash of cultures and civilizations. Samir closes with the question of what difference this letter will make in the Muslim world where Christians continue to be oppressed, Christian priests are kidnapped and apostates are persecuted. It is important, he says, that the next stages in dialogue focus on the issues of religious freedom, the absolute value of human rights, and the religious use of violence.[7]

From the various Orthodox churches there has been hardly any official response to the Muslim initiative. A Middle Eastern prelate complained that he had received no reply to his approaches from the 138 scholars, and concluded that they only wanted dialogue with Western Christians.

Metropolitan of All America Ukrainian Autocephalous Orthodox Church and Archbishop of New York, Mykhayil Javchak Champion. This Orthodox prelate noted the lack of Orthodox responses to the Muslim initiative, which he blames on indifference and insecurity. He would like to see Orthodoxy becoming more inclusive, both towards other Christians and towards other religions, including Islam. He welcomes the letter and its call for common ground on the theme of love for God and neighbor. He is encouraged by Muslim acceptance of

---

7   Samir Khalil Samir, "The Letter of 138 Muslim scholars to the Pope and Christian Leaders", October 17, 2007, http://www.asianews.it/index.php?l=en&art=10577viewed January 17, 2008.

Jesus as the Messiah (apparently he does not realize the term is used in the Qur'an). He agrees with the 138 Muslim scholars that the major truths of both religions are "made of the same stuff," so are actually not so different. He closes with reflections on the peaceful relations between Muslims and Christians in contemporary Ukraine.[8]

Archbishop Rowan Williams, Primate of all England and senior bishop of the worldwide Anglican Communion. While welcoming the Muslim letter as the basis for further development of dialogue and common action between Christians and Muslims, Williams tactfully indicated his concern for Christian minorities in the Muslim world:

> The theological basis of the letter and its call to 'vie with each other only in righteousness and good works; to respect each other, be fair, just and kind to another and live in sincere peace, harmony and mutual good will,' are indicative of the kind of relationship for which we yearn in all parts of the world, and especially where Christians and Muslims live together. It is particularly important in underlining the need for respect towards minorities in contexts where either Islam or Christianity is the majority presence.[9]

Bishop Mark Hanson, President of the Lutheran World Federation. Hanson gratefully welcomed the sincerity expressed by the Muslim authors, and their stress on a shared heritage in the "sacred texts of the Abrahamic faiths." He expresses a vaguely worded hope that Jews, Muslims and Christians will receive God's living revelation in the world without fear from their neighbors.[10]

---

8   Mykhayil Javchak Champion, "Reflection on 'A Common Ground Between Us and You,'" posted on the Official Website of A Common Word, http://www.acommonword.com/index.php?page=responses&item=46 viewed January 15, 2008.

9   Eric Young, "Muslim Peace Call to Christians Welcomed", *Christian Post*, http://www.christianpost.com/article/20071012/29671_Muslim_Peace_Call_to_Christians_Welcomed.htm viewed January 11, 2008; "Archbishop's response to *A Common Word*", The Official Website of A Common Word, http://www.acommonword.com/index.php?page=responses&item=11 viewed January 15, 2008.

10   "The text of the presiding bishop and LWF president", Evangelical Lutheran Church in America, posted on the Official Website of A Common Word, http://www.acommonword.com/index.php?page=responses&item=2 viewed January 15, 2008.

Evangelical Alliance, UK: General Director Joel Edwards welcomed the Muslim call to peaceful engagement between faiths. However, the EA statement acknowledges the abiding differences between the two faiths. "Neither Christianity, nor Islam, is built on an abstract notion of love or faith. Rather, Christianity is built upon the foundation of Jesus Christ, the God who became flesh and lived among us."[11]

Professor David Ford, Director of Cambridge University's Inter-Faith Program, warmly welcomed the letter as an unprecedented positive statement of friendship to Christians, a "historic template for the future . . . an astonishing achievement of solidarity, one that can be built on in the future."[12]

David Coffey, President of the Baptist World Alliance. Coffey welcomed the Muslim letter as a groundbreaking initiative which could make a major contribution to a better understanding in Christian-Muslim relations, the cause of religious liberty and global peace.[13]

However, he also expresses his concern for Christians, and those of other faiths, who are denied full religious liberty.

Zein al-Abdeen Al Rekabi, a Muslim scholar, published an article "An Opportunity to Discuss Our Knowledge of Mohammed and Jesus," in *Asharq Alawsat,* January 9, 2008. Responding to a call by the Archbishop of Canterbury to Muslims to learn about Christian culture, Al-Rekabi presents the traditional Muslim view that all that is worth knowing about Jesus is already found in Islam and is part of the Muslim faith. He supplies a list of quotations from the Qur'an and *hadith* concerning Jesus and his mother, Mary, and concludes that Muslims have an "extensive knowledge in their sources about Jesus, the Virgin Mary, the Bible and

---

11   Eric Young, "Muslim Peace Call to Christians Welcomed", *Christian Post*, October 12, 2007, http://www.christianpost.com/article/20071012/29671_Muslim_Peace_Call_to_Christians_Welcomed.htm viewed January 11, 2008.

12   "Muslim leaders' 'historic' statement of friendship welcomed", *University of Cambridge News and Events*, http://www.admin.cam.ac.uk/news/dp/2007101101 viewed January 11, 2008.

13   "Personal response from the BWA President to Letter from Muslim Scholars", posted on the Official Website of A Common Word, http://www.acommonword.com/index.php?page=responses&item=32 viewed January 15, 2008.

the venerated Apostles." So Muslims are not ignorant of Christianity. Rather, the need is for Christians to learn more about Islam and its tolerance. Al-Rekabi's view represents the common Muslim attitude, which claims that Islam has superseded Christianity and that Islamic source texts contain all that is worth knowing of the previous original but superseded revelations in the Jewish and Christian scriptures. These scriptures were later corrupted by Jews and Christians and are no longer reliable. Thus there is no need for Muslims to further gain any knowledge about contemporary Christianity.

Brief summary of responses

There appears to be a clear difference between Western Evangelical, and Catholic, Orthodox and non-Western Christian responses to the Muslim letter. Non-Western Christians are clearly worried for its implications on their precarious survival in Muslim-majority countries; mainline Catholics and Orthodox are more conservative in their theology, and realize the dangers and temptations of the Muslim approach. Ironically, the Evangelical response seems more in tune with a liberal ecumenical and inclusive interfaith approach, which comes close to accepting Islam as a legitimate way to God, Muhammad as a prophet of God and the Qur'an as a revelation from God.

Analysis of the Yale Statement

"The road to hell is paved with good intentions." (16th century proverb)

"Behold, I send you out as sheep in the midst of wolves; so be shrewd as serpents and innocent as doves." (Matthew 10:16, NASB)

Introduction

In the field of interreligious relations, symbols are very important. So is the recognition and respect for the basic differences in doctrine, theology and practice. While the search for common ground is important for forging a mutual drive towards peaceful relations, it must not come at the expense of the mutual respect for the other's specificity and the essential requirement of reciprocity and equality. An eagerness to grasp at the common ground presented by the Muslim letter is clearly evident in the Yale Statement, and it has seemingly blinded its authors to the negative implications of the Muslim letter. The Muslim leaders know of this desperate Christian longing for common ground, and manipulate it to their advantage.

The tone of the Muslim letter is condescending, given from a position of superiority and strength. It seems to imply that in spite of Christian guilt in fomenting war and aggression against Muslims, the Muslims scholars are offering Christians peace and harmony, if only they will accept the conditions laid down explicitly and implicitly in the document. The tone of the Yale response document, on the other hand, is one of abject humility, guilt and subjugation.

It is well known that for Islam, honor and power are of central importance. Islam, which sees itself as the last and final revelation of God to humanity, can brook no rivals. The traditional view is that God has exalted Islam and Muslims above all other religions and made them superior to all others. According to the Qur'an, Muslims are "The best of peoples, evolved for mankind" (Q 3:110). According to a well-known *hadith*, "Islam increases and does not diminish."[14] Other versions of this *hadith* state that "Islam is exalted and nothing is exalted above it." All relationships with non-Muslims have to serve the principle of the exaltation and strengthening of Islam and of Muslims as compared to non-Muslim communities. The term that best describes this relationship is **dominant-subordinate**: Muslims are dominant, all others are subordinate.

The Muslim scholars well understand the importance of symbols and terms, using every opportunity to elevate Islam and its founder, scripture and basic doctrines while denigrating those of Christianity.

---

14   *Sunan Abu-Dawood*, Beirut: Dar al-Fikr (Arabic), third part, book of obligations, gate: does the Muslim inherit from the kafir? Hadith 2912, (Vol. 2, p. 126).

The Christian scholars seem to have fallen into this trap, responding in what they seem to think is appropriate Islamic terminology, rather than Biblical and Christian theological terms, in an effort to please and appease Muslim sensibilities. This further denigrates Christianity and elevates Islam – one of the apparent aims of the Muslim endeavor.

This would seem to be the end result of the long road towards relativism in theology and theological contextualization, undertaken by some of the authors, in an effort to appear relevant to secular and multicultural interests in society and in mission. This stand would suggest to Muslims a weaker Christian position, which accepts Muslim superiority in religion. This is reminiscent of the traditional submissive role required of *dhimmi* minorities (Christians and Jews) within an Islamic state.

There is much confusion these days among Evangelicals. Some seem to be carrying the lapsed liberal agenda of the 1960s-1980s. They are watering down their adherence to basic Biblical doctrines and accepting post-modernist and Islamic perspectives on many issues. Some have acceded to the notion that Christian missions are, on the whole, programs of aggressive proselytization linked to the colonial era which should be forbidden. Aggressive proselytization is seen as an act of violence against Muslims from a position of power. In the Muslim view, Christian aid and development efforts are also part of the aggressive missionary program of Christianity and should be prohibited. This fits in well with the postmodern secularist agenda of eliminating truth and value content from all religions equally. In interfaith dialogue, Muslims have always attacked Christian evangelism as aggressive and hurtful to Muslims, without critiquing Muslim *da'wa*. Muslims always demand an end to Christian evangelism in Muslim states and in Muslim societies and minorities. They never promise to stop Islamic *da'wa* in return. This is just one example of the way in which some Evangelicals in the West are yielding more and more to such demands, resulting in a weakening of Christianity and an empowerment of Islam.

Did all the Evangelicals sign freely and willingly?

It appears that the authors of the Yale Statement managed to persuade some Evangelical leaders to sign the document without the signatories necessarily having a comprehensive knowledge of Islam and its attitudes and approaches to other religions.

Leith Anderson, President of the National Association of Evangelicals (NAE) admitted that he signed the Yale Statement because of pressure put on him by other leaders, although he was not happy with some of its contents, and although his request for some changes were not met. Evangelical leaders knowledgeable in Islam had encouraged him to sign it nevertheless. He did so because "there was simply no easy way to process the complexities of this inter-faith communiqué on short notice."

Is it possible that other Evangelical leaders may have been persuaded to sign against their better judgment? Anderson, in an attempt to limit the damage, added that his signature was given as an individual, not as the President of the NAE. He explained that he hopes the dialogue with Muslims will lead to mutual respect, freedom to state his specific faith without pretending to a comprehensive mutual agreement that does not exist, and religious liberty including that of conversion. He concluded that:

> As an evangelical Christian I believe in Jesus Christ as my Savior and Lord. I take the Bible seriously as my rule of faith and practice. That is who evangelicals are and what evangelicals believe. Just as Muslims want us to know about Islam I want Muslims to know about the Gospel of Jesus Christ.[15]

It is unfortunate he was not able to insist on including his reservations, hopes and beliefs in the document.

The understandable desire to respond positively and in love to the perceived olive branch presented by the Muslim scholars seems to have

---

15   Leith Anderson, "Signing the Letter to Islam", National Association of Evangelicals, November 20, 2007, http://www.nae.net/index.cfm?FUSEACTION=editor.page&pageID=500&IDcategory=1 viewed January 11, 2008.

overridden any sense of suspicion or of a deeper examination of the implications of the letter. It has been claimed by one of the authors that the Yale Statement would start a process which will culminate in reconciliation between Christianity and Islam. While we may pray for peace and harmony between Muslims and Christians in areas of physical conflict, there is no Biblical warrant for seeking reconciliation between Christianity and non-Christian religions such as Islam. Non-Christians are called to be reconciled to God by faith in Jesus Christ, outside of whom there is no salvation – this is the Biblical message. Watering down Christian fundamental doctrines and accepting Muslim claims to effect a hoped for reconciliation with Muslims can only lead to syncretism.

The marginalization of Christ and the Bible

The Muslim scholars in their open letter respectfully call Muhammad "the Prophet Muhammad," adding the compulsory PBUH (Peace Be Upon Him) after every mention of his name, placing him immediately after God in the opening invocation: "In the Name of God, the Compassionate, the Merciful, And may peace and blessings be upon the Prophet Muhammad," as well as quoting the *shahada*: "There is no god but God, Muhammad is the messenger of God" in which Muhammad is again mentioned immediately after God. The Christian scholars on the other hand, have denigrated and marginalized the person of our Lord and Savior Jesus Christ, merely referring to Him as "Jesus Christ" as the Muslim scholars have done, as though he were just a mere human being with no special status for Christians. There is no allusion to his deity and lordship. There is no exaltation of his person and rank. It would seem he is not even a prophet with the status Muhammad has for Muslims. They have thus inadvertently confirmed the Muslim view of the superiority of Muhammad over Jesus.

There is a similar disparity in the treatment of the respective scriptures. The Muslim scholars respectfully call their scripture "the Holy Qur'an" whenever it is mentioned. The Christian scholars, on the other hand, simply refer to "the New Testament" rather than to "The Holy Bible."

It would seem that for the Christian scholars the basics of their religion are no longer to be treated as holy, precious and respected. This appears to substantiate the idea that the Yale Statement was influenced by liberal Christianity which has long since abandoned its faith in the fundamental doctrines of the Christian religion. This suggests a definite shift from orthodox Christian doctrine to a pluralist stand that denies the exclusivity of Christ in God's plan of salvation and downplays orthodox Christian views on the Trinity, the person of Christ, and the authority of the Bible.

Another possibility is that some of the authors and signatories of the letter are so strongly motivated by their concern for evangelism among Muslims that they have gone beyond the acceptable contextualization of form (adopting Muslim forms and language for Christian worship) to an unacceptable contextualization of theology, thus accepting Muslim claims to the prophethood of Muhammad and the revelatory nature of the Qur'an.

The Yale Statement problematically uses the term "Prophet" to designate Muhammad. Do the authors of the letter and the signatories really accept Muhammad as a true prophet of God? If so, then logically they should follow Muhammad's teachings and the revelation he claimed to have brought, i.e. they should be Muslims. If they firmly believe in the finality of God's revelation in Christ, then Muhammad is either no prophet at all or a false prophet and it would be wrong to give Muslims the impression that Christians accept his status as a true prophet of God. A better term would have been "Muhammad the founder of Islam" or something similar. If reciprocity is asked for in this dialogue, than the Muslim scholars should have used a Christian title of Jesus such as "Lord" or "Savior" which they did not do. So why should Christians give Muhammad his Muslim designation of "Prophet"?

Agreeing to the Muslim concept of love of God and love of one's neighbor

The authors of the Yale Statement have affirmed the Muslim statement that love of God and love of neighbor are at the heart of Islam, as they are in Christianity. However, the whole tenor of the Muslim document proves that what is really central to Islam is the monolithic unity of God that denies the deity of Christ, and the status of Muhammad as the final and only valid prophet and messenger of God, thus denying the finality of God's revelation in Christ. They claim that these two testimonies are "the *sine qua non* of Islam." This is the real subtext of the Muslim letter, and anyone trained in Islamic studies should have been able to spot it immediately. It is a sad reflection on the Christian leaders who authored the Yale document that they either knowingly ignored these implications or else did not notice them. In either case they are disqualified from speaking in the name of a vast number of Christians who still believe in the orthodox Christian teachings on Christ, the Trinity and the Holy Bible. A more appropriate response would have been a reiteration of the basic Christian doctrines of the deity of Christ, of the Trinity and of the finality of God's revelation in Christ as the central doctrines of the Christian faith, coupled with the revelation of God as love. Ignoring the Muslim subtext seems to imply that the Christians acknowledge the correctness of the Muslim claims.

The Anglican Bishop of London, Richard Chartres, in his response to the Muslim letter states:

> This is a substantial letter which speaks of the unity of God from a Muslim perspective. It demands a substantial response which approaches the same theme from a Christian perspective.[16]

The Yale authors would have done well to heed his recommendation. The Muslim letter indeed calls for a response which clarifies the Christian orthodox position on these themes. Only from such a clear statement of Christian positions can progress be made in dialogue towards a reconciliation that fully accepts the right of the other to be different without suffering any disadvantage for it.

---

16 "Response from the Bishop of London to the Open Letter from 138 Muslim scholars and addressed to the spiritual leaders of the Christian world", The Official Website of A Common Word, http://www.acommonword.com/index.php?page=responses&item=4 viewed January 15, 2008.

The Aal al-Bayt Institute conference on "Love in the Holy Qur'an"

In September 2007, the Royal Aal al-Bayt Institute for Islamic Thought in Amman, Jordan, held a conference on the topic "Love in the Holy Qur'an" to prepare the ground for the October 2007 letter by Muslim scholars addressed to Christian leaders. One of the 32 papers offered at this conference was "Differences between the Muslim and the Christian Concept of Divine Love" by the German convert to Islam, Dr. Murad Wilfried Hofmann. This paper defines the concept of love for God and neighbor in Islam in terms very similar to those used in the Barnabas Fund analysis of the Muslim letter. (The paper is reproduced in Appendix 1.)

Hofmann states that the Muslim concept of love for God differs from the Christian concept because Muslims do not accept that God was incarnated in a human Jesus. He repeats the traditional orthodox Muslim views on God as wholly transcendent, "The One beyond time and space Whose Being totally escapes our categorization . . . He remains unfathomable, unimaginable, unseizable, incomprehensible, indescribable." God's attributes, as presented in the 99 Beautiful names, are "of little help, because we must not coin any similitudes for God (6:74)." God can only be defined in negative terms, listing what cannot be said of Him. For Muslims, loving God is only "naively possible." Sufi attempts at developing an Islamic mysticism of love are appreciated, but they face the difficulties of visualizing God, which is forbidden. The Sufi approach, while emotionally more satisfactory than the sobriety of the philosophical approach, is described as highly speculative (carrying the nuance that it is not to be trusted or followed).[17]

Hofmann also states that the self-sufficiency of God precludes describing him as loving his creation, for a love relationship includes dependency which is inconceivable in God. Loving his creation is "incompatible with

---

17   Dr. Murad Wilfried Hofmann, "Differences between the Muslim and the Christian Concept of Divine Love", Royal Aal al-Bayt Institute for Islamic Thought, The 14th General Conference, Amman, September 4-7, 2007, Amman: The Hashemite Kingdom of Jordan, pp. 5-6.

the very nature of God as sublime and totally self-sufficient." He admits that the Qur'an states that God "loves" the good and the just. He gives a list of those God loves:[18]

- the doers of good (Q 3: 31, 148; 5: 93)
- those who are patient in adversity (Q 3: 146)
- those who place their trust in Him (Q 3: 159)
- those who are conscious of Him (Q 9: 7)
- all who purify themselves (Q 9: 108)
- those who believe and do perform good deeds (Q 19: 96)
- those who act equitably (Q 60: 8)

However, the Qur'an also lists those God does not love:

- the disbelievers (Q 3: 32)
- the transgressors (Q 5: 87; 7: 55)
- the wasteful (Q 7: 31)
- the traitors (Q 8: 58)

While Hofmann does not state it, it is worth mentioning that Christians and Jews, though "people of the book," are nevertheless often described by orthodox Islam as composing one category of the totality of disbelievers (*kafirun*) because they reject the final prophethood of Muhammad and God's revelation given to him in the Qur'an. They are therefore not loved by God, but rather disliked by him.

According to Hofmann, Muslims are hesitant about using the term "love" and prefer to use the term "brotherhood" in relations with other humans.[19] Hofmann also admits that the concept of loving one's enemy is purely Christian, it is simply not found in Islam.[20]

Another paper presented at the conference is that by Arif Kamal, Pakistani

---

18 Dr. Murad Wilfried Hofmann, "Differences between the Muslim and the Christian Concept of Divine Love", pp. 7-9.

19 Dr. Murad Wilfried Hofmann, "Differences between the Muslim and the Christian Concept of Divine Love", pp. 7-8.

20 Dr. Murad Wilfried Hofmann, "Differences between the Muslim and the Christian Concept of Divine Love", p. 10.

Ambassador to Jordan, 2003-2007.[21] Kamal claims that those human beings who act justly, are pure and perform righteous deeds are worthy of attracting God's love. This presupposes that all others are not. According to Kamal, God's love is the result of human effort at establishing a just society. Human action comes first; God's love is a response to human initiative. Muslims are commanded to love their brothers – in this context, brothers seems to indicate fellow Muslims. How different are these ideas from the Biblical concept of God's love poured on unmeriting, unworthy and sinful human beings; of God taking the initiative in first loving us unconditionally.

It would be interesting to know whether the authors of the Yale Statement had read these papers, which are available on the Aal al-Bayt website.[22] It seems clear that the concept of love in Islam, as explained by Hofmann and Kamal, is very different from that in Christianity. The claim in the Muslim letter that the concept of love is identical in both religions is therefore strange, to say the least.

We as Christians are called to love our enemy, turn the other cheek, humble ourselves and serve. Muslims are not. In Christianity, God is love and love is central and unconditional; not so in Islam.

Assuming responsibility and guilt for the Crusades and the war on terror

The authors of the Yale Statement assume responsibility both for the Crusades and for the contemporary war on Islamic terrorism in the name of all Christians. In this they again reinforce Muslim attitudes of seeing all non-Muslims as one bloc, one *umma* according to the well-known Muslim adage: *al-kufar kullahu milatun wahida* (the unbelievers are all one nation).[23] The individual is recognized only in his connection to the community he belongs to, he has no value in himself as a free individual before God, created in God's image.

---

21 Arif Kamal, " 'Hubb' and the Human Endeavour: Love as a Foundation for Community in the Abrahamic Tradition", Royal Aal al-Bayt Institute for Islamic Thought, The 14th General Conference, Amman, September 4-7, 2007, Amman: The Hashemite Kingdom of Jordan.

22 http://www.aalalbayt.org/en/respapers.html#rd22

23 Al-Shafi'i, *Kitab al-umm*, vol. 4, p. 261, II. 2-3; Ibn Kathir, *Tafsir*, vol. 7, p. 393.

This communal view of human society still underpins Muslim responses to non-Muslims, as has been clearly evident in the angry and often violent responses to the Rushdie affair, to the Danish Muhammad cartoons and to the Pope's lecture at Regensburg. This follows the view that if one non-Muslim transgresses, the whole non-Muslim community worldwide is responsible and must be punished until it compensates and appeases the Muslims for the offence. This has always been the attitude taken towards *dhimmis* in Muslim states. It is not the individual who is punished after due legal process, but the whole community to which he nominally belongs is subjected to violence, until its leaders humble themselves before the Muslims and compensate them for the perceived offence. For most Muslims, all nominal Christians worldwide still form one community, and Christians in Muslim states still suffer persecution and violence for any perceived offence against Islam committed by any nominally Christian person or institution in other lands.

The acceptance by some Christians - mainly Westerners - of communal historical guilt thus reinforces Muslim trends to punish indigenous Christians in Muslim lands – who were not consulted about making the apology - for all the supposed sins against Islam ever perpetrated by any so-called Christian or Christians throughout history. This has been forcefully evident in recent years in places such as Iraq, Indonesia, Sudan, Nigeria and elsewhere. The acceptance of corporate Christian guilt by the Yale authors will inevitably have detrimental effects on Christians in Muslim-majority societies everywhere, who even now are suffering for their loyalty to Christ.

While some Christians hold that the involvement of Christians, and especially of the Catholic Church, in the Crusades was contrary to the teachings of the Lord Jesus Christ, many recognize that there was a need to defend the vulnerable Christians of the Holy Land. Thus the First Crusade was an understandable (possibly justifiable) belated response to the initial Muslim aggression in the first expansionist *jihad* which conquered and subjugated vast Christian regions and which posed a continuing threat to Christians in the Middle East and to Europe itself. Subsequent Crusades were, however, less easy to justify, and, with regard to behavior, sadly both sides fought according to the norms of the time, shocking though it seems today. Apologies on behalf of all Christians ring hollow for those Middle Eastern Christians, such as the Armenians and Assyrians, who have faced genocide at the hands of Islamic armies and fanatics. Furthermore, such apologies simply harden Muslim attitudes of self-righteousness, confirming their conviction that they are guilty of no wrongdoing. This issue should have been left for further discussions with Muslim leaders where reciprocal mutual penitence and forgiveness could be shared.

Muslims have welcomed the apology in the Yale Statement and reported it widely on their websites, noting how Christians have finally admitted to their wrongdoings. There does not seem to be any reference to any Muslim violence, either past or present, which Muslims might need to apologize for.

Claiming that Christians are responsible for the excesses in the "war on terror" again reinforces Muslim perceptions of the responses of Western states to Islamist terrorism as a Christian war against Islam. This is fueled by Muslim conspiracy theories about an ancient and still current worldwide Christian conspiracy (allied to Jews) to destroy Islam. Unless the authors of the Yale Statement agree with these Muslim misconceptions, they should at the very least have clarified the issues. This would include explaining that Western states are secular, not Christian entities, and that the "war on terror" is mainly a political and military response of secular states to attacks upon them and their citizens.

The Muslim scholars state in "A Common Word":

> When freedom to worship God according to one's conscience is curtailed, God is dishonored, the neighbor oppressed, and neither God nor neighbor is loved.

This is clearly a statement we would all agree to. However, the Yale authors miss this opportunity to demand that Muslims live up to this claim and practice what they preach. Britain has over 1700 mosques for its approximately 3 million Muslims; similar numbers of mosques exist in France, Germany and the USA. Saudi Arabia does not permit even one church for almost a million Christians residing in it, yet a number of Saudi Wahhabi scholars signed the Muslim letter. In most Muslim states, Christians face humiliating restrictions on building and repairing churches, and on public expressions of Christianity and its symbols. Muslims in the West do not usually face such restrictions. Similar inequalities can be multiplied. The effects of the Islamic Law of Apostasy, which has not been repealed by Muslim scholars, are felt by many Muslim converts to Christianity who are severely persecuted everywhere in the Muslim world and even in Western states, while converts to Islam are given recognition and have total freedom and security in the West. Muslims are free to propagate Islam in the West, yet Christian mission is severely restricted, if not totally forbidden, in most Muslim states. Is it not the grave responsibility of Christian leaders to seize every opportunity to redress these wrongs and help their suffering brothers and sisters in Muslim countries who are usually powerless to help themselves?

The Yale authors express the desire for future meetings between Muslim and Christian leaders at every level to implement the expressed principle of love for God and neighbor. Are they ready for the first demand that will be made by Muslim leaders, namely that Christians cease all evangelistic efforts aimed at Muslims as a sign of their goodwill? It is well known that Christian mission to Muslims is viewed as aggression against Islam, while Islamic *da'wa* is viewed as the God-ordained command and right of Muslims everywhere. There seems to be a trend in current Evangelical missions to differentiate between permitted evangelism and forbidden proselytism. Muslims are cleverly redefining most forms of

Christian outreach as proselytism and have succeeded in branding it as unacceptable in the Western media, academia and certain Christian circles. The emerging scenario around the world is of Christian missions being increasingly limited both by secular states and in Muslim lands, while Muslim *da'wa* activities are rapidly advancing and expanding worldwide. How can Christians face the advance of militant Islam when Christianity has become so fragmented in its approach to Islam? In spite of the peaceable rhetoric within "A Common Word," Islam is still a one-way-street in its practical relations with Christians and other non-Muslims living in its midst.

Conclusion

Currently Christian responses to Islam are many and various. Some suggest that there are two opposing positions: one is to embrace Islamic ideals and the other is to regard Islam itself as intrinsically evil and to have nothing to do with it. But Barnabas Fund believes that there is a third way for Christians to meet with Muslims, recognizing that there are two main areas for discussion. One area has to do with Muslims and Christians living in society and the other has to do with theology and spirituality. Barnabas Fund's belief is that the latter is not the priority in our world today. We must recognize that there are vital differences in theology between Islam and Christianity which are unbridgeable, and therefore discussions on theology can never be very productive although they can result in increased understanding and respect for each other. It is the discussion of Muslims and Christians living in society which is the priority and indeed the urgency, and from which practical and positive change can be expected. Therefore, as the Pope has set out, discussion with Muslims must include full equality, human rights and religious liberty for Christian minorities; liberty to comprise not only freedom of worship but also the freedom to share the Christian faith and to convert to it.

The Christian leaders in the Yale Statement are in effect giving everything away without receiving anything in return. The Muslim scholars have succeeded in dividing Christians among themselves, thus weakening the Church and empowering Islam. While the Muslim scholars have created an unprecedented united front and consensus among Muslims, they have managed to divide Christianity as never before. The negative effects of this letter will be felt foremost by the indigenous Christians in Muslim-majority states and societies who are already suffering from various forms of Muslim pressure, harassment and outright persecution. The Yale Statement does not deal with the serious issue of human rights and religious freedom as it affects Christian minorities and as enshrined in Article 18 of the United Nations Universal Declaration of Human Rights.

Current interfaith dialogue has inherent risks that must be clearly grasped before getting involved:

1. There is a risk that Christians will do all the giving and Muslims all the taking. This is inherent in the very nature of the two religions. Christianity stresses meekness, humility, confession, repentance, sacrifice and self-denial. Islam prizes power, domination and honor. Humility and meekness of the other side are seen as shameful and as signs of weakness to be seized upon and utilized. Muslims find it very difficult to accept blame because of the shame, humiliation and loss of face implied. Muslims will usually present their case as victims, make accusations against Christianity and demand compensatory actions. At the same time they will fiercely resist any discussion of Muslim shortcomings such as the bloody history of *jihad* and the persecution of Christians in Muslim states.

2. Muslims often engage in dialogue with the aim of *da'wa,* or converting others. Both religions believe in mission. Most Christians are happy to see it as a two-way process, with each faith having the freedom to propagate its message and try to convince

others. Muslims see *da'wa* as a one–way street: only Islam as the God-given, final and true revelation has the right to propagate itself. Christians only have the limited right of worship within their churches. Muslims reject all Christian mission endeavours and seek to suppress them and smear them as deceitful and evil.

3. Christians present themselves as vulnerable and are open about their views, attitudes and aims. Muslims have a long tradition of using *taqiyya* (dissimulation, deceit) when in positions of inferiority and weakness, sanctioned by religious doctrine. Using different discourses to different audiences is fully acceptable in Muslim practice. What is said one day in a specific context might be totally contradicted by what the same leaders might say another day in another context. Muslim rhetorical statements and joint declarations with Christians thus have limited value, as most Muslims understand the hidden agendas behind them.

4. Certain key vocabularies are understood differently by Muslims. There is a great risk of misunderstanding and of talking at cross purposes. For example, the word "peace" for Muslims carries the connotation of establishing peace and order by spreading Islamic rule and authority across the globe. In the Muslim letter the word "love" is used in Islam to express God's monolithic unity (*tawhid*) and the obligation to obey it implicitly to gain his favor, rather than the Christian view of the Triune God's unlimited and unconditional love to sinners. Similarly, when Muslims claim that Islamic societies were historically tolerant of non-Muslims, they mean that non-Muslims were not killed or expelled but allowed to live and continue to practice their non-Muslim faith on condition they observed the restrictions of *dhimmi* status. This is very different from the modern Western Christian understanding of tolerance as implying full equality.

Sadly, it would seem that the Catholic response to the Muslim letter is more sensitive to the real issues facing Muslim-Christian relations than is the Yale Statement. Catholics have taken the issue of the social context of religious freedom and human rights within Muslim societies very seriously, especially as they relate to vulnerable Christian minorities. The Yale authors appear to have missed or ignored the Muslim subtext and its implicit message, and the reality of Christian suffering in Muslim lands. Are these Christian minorities to be sacrificed again to the self-interest of Western Christians?

APPENDIX 1
Dr. Murad Wilfried Hofmann,
"Differences between the Muslim and the Christian Concept of Divine Love"*

The 14th General Conference
Amman, September 4-7, 2007

Differences between the Muslim and the
Christian Concept of Divine Love
Dr. Murad Wilfried Hofmann
Amman- The Hashemite Kingdom of Jordan

1. Introduction

All religions fulfill several functions. They try to establish a relationship between man and the larger Reality of which he forms a tiny part, orienting him within the immense universe that he inhabits.

This usually [1] leads to a metaphysical interpretation of the world and conceptionally to the postulation of a divine Supreme Being. These efforts sooner or later culminate in a science of God, verbally "theology," called *al-aqida* in Islam.

---

* http://www.aalalbayt.org/ar/ResearchDocuments/14.pdf viewed May 3, 2008.

In everyday life religions are also called upon to provide rules for worshiping the Deity (al-'ibadat) and for the conduct of human affairs in all fields (al-mu'amalat). These aspects of religiosity tend to command the greatest attention, not only because they impact directly on the conduct of everyday life, but also because they are more concrete and practical than the rather esoteric contributions of theology in its original and purest sense.

Worse, the role played by religions in politics today begets activities which totally overshadow the theological aspects of religion. This is true of all contemporary religious or pseudo–religious phenomena known as "-isms."

They include American Evangelical Christians promoting a frighteningly politicized fundamentalism as well as what now is called Islamism, i.e., a militant political ideology practiced by Muslims. [2]

Therefore, as recognized by the Royal Aal al-Bayt Institute for Islamic Thought, it is now of the essence to focus on the very root of Islamic religiosity: the belief in Allah *ta'ala* as a Deity Who interacts with His creation in a *loving* manner and Who commands the *love* and affection of all true believers.

2. Loving God in Islam and Christianity

1. The Christian Concept

Christians consider their faith prototypically a "religion of love." This is meant comprehensively, i.e. as a religious appeal, and even command, (a) to love God and (b) to love "one's neighbor," i.e. all of mankind - friends and enemies as well.

a. Loving God:

The Christian command to love God, announced by Jesus, is embedded in St. Mark 12:30 and reads: **And you shall love the Lord, your God, with all your soul, and with all your mind, and with all your strength; this is the first commandment.**

In the words of Hugo Ball (d. 1927) the faithful are not on the look-out for reasons justifying the love of God. Rather, they "throw themselves into the love of God like pearl fishers diving into the ocean." [3]

In reality, this command is not a Christian innovation at all. The same text - verbally - figured already in the Fifth Book of Moses 6,5. Indeed, according to the Bible God is not only lovable for being gracious, just and merciful.

Indeed, the Book of Songs - being the 5th Book of the Biblical Psalms - is a treasure of lines professing love of God. No wonder the Church incorporated the Psalms into Christian lore, just as the Muslims have adopted them (calling them az-zabur) as one of the few reliably revealed passages of the Old Testament:

I love the Lord because He has heard my voice and my supplication (116:1).

Gracious is the Lord, and righteous, yes, our God is merciful (116:5).

Your commandments which I love shall be my delight (119:47).

Oh, how I love your law (119:97). **Your commands I have taken as a heritage forever, for they are the rejoicing of my heart** (119:111).

It will be noticed that the authors of the Psalms well before the Medieval Christian mystics had already reached a level of adoration where loving God and obeying his commands did no longer result from fear but from devotion.

The (unknown) author of the First Epistle of John 4 enlarges on this command by saying that God is love. He who dwells in love, dwells in God (4, 16).

b. *Loving man:*

The Christian command to love God is intimately linked to the "second command," i.e. to love one's fellow man:

And the second command is alike, namely this: You shall love your neighbor like yourself. There is no other command greater than these (St. Mark 12:31).

In the Book of Mormon this command reappears: Every man should love his neighbor as himself (Mosiah 23:15).

Insightful the great Jesuit theologian Karl Rahner (d. 1984) commented this rule as follows: "Love of God can only be realized through unconditional love of one's next-door neighbor since only that way one can pierce the hell of one's egotism." [5]

The Gospel makes clear that charity given to one's brother is a way of loving God:

In as much as you have done it to the least of my brothers, you have done it to Me (St. Matthew 25:40).

This is followed up by a statement of psychological depth:

"If a man should say 'I love God' but hates his brother, he is a liar. For if he does not love his brother whom he has seen, how can he love God Whom he has not seen?" (1 John 4:20).

c. *Peculiarities:*

In two ways the Christian concept of love is peculiar:

i. The Christian notion of loving God is deeply colored by the Christian doctrine of Incarnation which since the 1st Ecumenical Council of Ephesus in 325 implies that Jesus inseparably was both divine and human, figuring among the three divine persons who according to Church dogma form Trinity.

Consequently, for Christians the love of God is identified very much with loving Jesus, i.e. a concrete and therefore "touchable" historic personality.

Thus an encyclopedic definition of Christendom reads: "Love, faithfully having become visible in Jesus Christ, is the way towards hope for mankind." Romano Guardini (d. 1968) went to an extreme when formulating that "Jesus Christ is the essence of Christianity - not an idea, not a program, not an ideology, but a person." [6]

This notion is retained in the Book of Mormon where we read **"you must press forward with a steadfastness in Christ, having a perfect brightness of hope and a love of God and of all men."** (2 Nephi 31:20).

2. The Muslim Concept

a. Loving God

i. The climate of the Muslim devotion to God differs from the Christian one because for Muslims God has not been incarnated as Baby Jesus in the manger - cuddly and lovely - but rather remains an awesome Divinity, so close to us that we cannot see Him.

No human vision can encompass Him, whereas He encompasses all human vision (6:103).

In short, He is the One beyond time and space Whose Being totally escapes our categorization. Indeed, we cannot catch His Reality with the perceptional network provided by our man-made (and therefore "loaded" languages).

In fact, talking about God is a linguistic trap. Ludwig Wittgenstein (d. 1951) was therefore right in terminating his *Tractatus logico-philosophicus* (first printed in 1921) with the stunning phrase: "Of what one cannot speak, about that one must remain silent" (no. 7).

ii. True, for Muslims, too, Allah is not only transcendent but also immanent since Allah is closer to us than our jugular vein (50:16). And He has full knowledge of what is in the hearts (or bosoms) of people (11:5; 42:24; 57:6; 64:4; 67:13).

Muslims are therefore expected **to love Allah more than anything else** (2:165).

Nevertheless He remains unfathomable, unimaginable, unseizable, incomprehensible, indescribable. We are told that His are the most beautiful names / attributes (7:180; 17:110; 20:8). But this is of little help because we must not coin any similitudes for God (6:74).

It is of course true as well that in the Qur'an, for instance in the Light Verse (24:35) and in the Throne Verse (59:22-24) Allah has given us a self-description. Yet, do we really come closer to the secret when Allah identifies with the Light of the heavens and the earth? Can we understand any of the divine attributes other than nominalistically, like Ibn Hazm before?

Indeed, for he to whom Allah gives no light, no light whatever has he (24:40).

Therefore, we can legitimately go about defining God in negative terms only, listing what cannot be said of Him: That He cannot not exist; cannot die; cannot multiply Himself since God is a single God (2:163; 16:22, 51).

iii. All this is true and full of complexity. Nevertheless, loving God naively is possible not only for Christians but for Muslims as well since they are aware that **Allah in his goodness is limitless** (57:21) and that His **grace overspreads everything** (7:156).

All Muslims have to be grateful that Muslim mystics - the Sufi movement - have been able on this basis to develop an Islamic mysticism of love in spite of all the difficulties of visualizing Allah. The Sufi approach is of course highly speculative. But emotionally it is more satisfactory than the cool soberness of the philosophical (*al-mu-takalim*) approach described above.

b. Loving Man

As much as the Christian faith Islam teaches that the love of God must translate into compassion for man. However, Muslims are a bit more hesitant when it goes to use the word "love." In general they prefer to designate the same attitude as brother- and sisterhood.

Statements on brotherhood in the Qur'an most explicitly refer to relations between Muslims (3:103; 9:11; 48:29; 49:10). Even so, the Qur'an amply makes clear that its basic message is addressed to all of mankind (20:55; 40:64; 103; 114), not only by addressing its audience "Oh mankind!"or "Oh Children of Adam" (2:169; 4:170, 174; 7:26, 31, 35; 10:23, 57, 104, 108; 22:5; 31:33; 35:5, 15; 49:13; 53:3). Indeed the Qur'an is a clear lesson for all men and a guidance and an admonition for all the God-conscious (3:138).

As far as Christians are concerned the Qur'an does not pronounce an abstract concept like to "love your neighbor." However, in more concrete terms its verses establish that what is meant is the Christian way. Thus Muslims are urged to do good to their neighbors (4:36), show kindness even to (non-aggressive) disbelievers (60:8), spend on others in charity out of what one cherishes most (3:92; 4:114), and to be just in all dealings, no matter with whom (4:58; 5:8, 42; 7:29; 16: 90; 68:34).

If not in wording, in substance these rules add up to a Muslim "love thy neighbor"- command. By ruling out injustice, globally, Islam is commanding justice, globally.

3. God loving His creation in Islam and Christianity

1. The Christian Concept

a. The idea that God might "love" what He created is not self evident. On the contrary, one might argue that love establishes a longing and dependency between the lover and the loved one that is irreconcilable with God.

It seems feasible for the gods of Greek and Roman antiquity to pose as goddesses of love and beauty, like Aphrodite and Venus, because in antique mythology human love was a quality of gods.

b. Given the dual nature of Jesus in the eyes of Christians, his love for mankind may be understood more easily by them as corresponding to the human sentiment which all men and women experience. The same conclusion might be drawn from interpreting the history of Israel as a sentimental mutual relationship between a loving God and his privileged "Chosen People."

c. At any rate, in Christianity the loving nature of God is taken as an essential quality of deity, as expressed in startling fashion in 1 John 4:19:

We love Him because He first loved us.

On this basis Jesus is seen by many Christians as sort of a perfect Sufi. In fact, in much of Christian mysticism was cultivated a startling intimacy with Jesus that for Muslims borders on, or crosses over into, blasphemy.

This was true in particular with the Spanish nun St. Theresa of Avila (d.1582) and her spiritual friend St. John of the Cross (d. around 1581).

This trend opened the door for a humanization of Jesus, allowing him to be depicted as suffering with man, even now.

2. The Islamic Concept

a. In the Qur'an we are told that Allah is self-sufficient (64:6, last sentence). This fundamental self-description definitely excludes that Allah is in love with his creation the way humans treasure, desire, and miss each other, trying to fuse their self with a beloved person to whom they may become utterly dependent.

God cannot possibly love his creation that human way! Therefore it is safer and more accurate not to speak of "love" when addressing His clemency, compassion, benevolence, goodness, or mercy.

b. This assessment is not contradicted by the many verses in which Allah ta'ala is mentioned as "loving" something. Thus it says that Allah loves

- the doers of good (3:31, 148; 5:93),
- those who are patient in adversity (3:146),
- those who place their trust in Him (3:159),
- those who are conscious of Him (9:7)
- all who purify themselves (9:108)
- those who believe and do perform good deeds (19:96),
- those who act equitably (60:8).

In all these cases Allah "loves" must be understood as Allah "approves", "is content with" or "views positively" those who act as described. "Love" here does not refer to emotional involvement.

That this interpretation is correct can be deduced as well from those verses in which Allah speaks of not loving. Thus we read that Allah does not love:

- the disbelievers (3:32),
- the transgressors (5:87; 7:55),
- the wasteful (7:31), nor
- the traitors (8:58).

"Not loving" here stands for disapproving, condemning, criticizing, rejecting.

c. However, in 19:96 we do read after all that the Most Gracious will bestow His love on those who attain to faith and do good deeds, in 3:31 that If you indeed love Allah ... Allah will love you, and in 5:54 that, under circumstances, God will in time bring forth people whom He loves and who love Him. Admittedly, these quotations could be seen as proof for a love of God for His creation comparable to the love human beings are capable of. But this interpretation must be ruled out as incompatible with the very nature of God as sublime and totally self-sufficient.

4. Conclusion

1. The Christian and the Islamic considerations concerning love in divine context have been shown as not being identical but similar, as was to be expected.

2. Differences between the two approaches result above all from the
   • Muslim reticence to associate God with a humanized notion of love,
   • Muslim preference for the term "brotherhood" in most cases for which Christians choose to employ the term "love" (of one's neighbor).

3. There is, however, a major theoretical discrepancy between the two denominations in as much as the concept of loving one's enemy is nowhere to be found in Islamic doctrine (if one neglects certain Christianized Muslim mystic circles).

   This difference is, however, more theoretical than real. Indeed, at no moment in history was Christian behavior on the ground determined by their doctrine of loving one's enemy - not even to the slightest degree. And this observation is not surprising since loving one's enemy goes against the very grain of people and therefore is no-where acted upon as a rule. Living according to the concept of loving one's enemy was given only to a few people of saintly disposition, like St. Francis of Assisi (d. 1226) on the Christian side and Jalal ad-Din Rumi (d. 1273) among Muslims. Their supreme humility and tolerance, their devotion to other men, and their joyous religious fervor were so singular that, as exceptions, they confirmed the rule sketched out above.

4. This leads me to a final consideration concerning the psychological impact of promoting a rule - to love one's foe - that is inaccessible to 99.9% of all people.

Admitting this situation Christians might argue that nevertheless we need lofty ideals to strive for, even if they are virtually unattainable.

Muslims might reply that it is detrimental for public morality if unattainable rules are promoted which, of course, are constantly violated by everybody in sight, because that (Christian) approach creates a climate of, and promotes, hypocrisy at a massive scale. I share the latter judgment, being afraid that people used to violating basic rules of their professed moral code might become cynical about morality as such. Indeed there is divine wisdom behind the fact that all religious obligations placed on Muslims while not being easy to fulfill are all within reach of the average believer.

In this sense, too, Islam by being more simple is more sane.

End Notes

1. Buddhism is an exception in as much as Buddhists refuse entering into any speculation about transcendental reality. See Bukkyo Dendo Kyokai, The Teaching of Buddha, 9th ed., Kosaido Printing Co., Ltd.: Tokyo 2004.

2. The latter phenomenon has recently been diagnosed by Meghnad Desai, a British Lord, in his book on "Rethinking Islamism - the Ideology of the New Terror," Tauris: London 2007.

3. Hugo Ball, p. 49.

4. The author of this letter is unknown. He certainly was not the favorite disciple of Jesus known under the name of John.

5. Karl Rahner, Warum bin ich Christ? in: Meyers Enzyklopädisches Lexikon, Vol. 5, p. 672.

6. For both quotations (my translation) see Meyers (Note 5), p. 671

Bibliography Holy Scripts

a) Qur'an Translations

Le Saint Coran, King Fahd Complex: al-Madinah, KSA (n.d.) 'Ali, 'Abdullah Yusuf, Transl., The Meaning of the Holy Qur'an, 8th ed, amana publication: Beltsville, MD

Ansari, Zafar Ishaq, Transl., Towards Understanding the Qur'an, Abridged version of Sayyid Abul A'la Mawdudi's Tafhim al-Qur'an, The Islamic Foundation: Markfield, LE, 2006.

Asad, Muhammad, Transl., The Message of the Qur'an, 2nd ec., The Book Foundation: Bitton, Bristol, UK 2003

Bewley, Abdalhaqq and Aisha, Transl., The Noble Qur'an, Bookwork: Nor-wich 1999

Max Henning / Murad Wilfried Hofmann, Transl., Der Koran, 4th ed., Die- derichs: München 2005

Pickthall, Marmaduke (1930), Transl., Cagri Yayinlari: Istanbul 2002

b) Christian Scripts

Bibel, Die, German translation, Naumann & Göbel: Cologne 1984

Book of Mormon, The, The Church of Jesus Christ of Latterday Saints: Salt Lake City, Utah, USA 1981

Holy Bible, The Gideons International: Nashville, Tennessee 37214 (n.d.)

New Testament, The, Verbreitung der Heiligen Schrift: D-6345 Eschenburg 1 (n.d.)

Literature

Abdou, Cheikh Mohammed, Rissalat al Tawhid, Paul Geuthner: Paris 1925

Asad, Muhammad, Islam at the Crossroads, Sh. Muhammad Ashraf: Lahore 1934

Ball, Hugo, Byzantinisches Christentum, 2nd ed., Insel Verlag: Frankfurt 1979

Brunner-Traut, Emma, Die Kopten, DG 39, 4th ed., Diederichs Verlag: München 1993

Ceric, Mustafa, Roots of Synthetic Theology in Islam, I.I.I.T.(ISTAC): Kuala Lumpur 1995

Franziskus von Assisi, Works, German transl., 3rd ed., Werl 1963

Hoßfeld, Paul, Moses- Zarathustra- Buddha- Jesus- Mani- Mohammed, Bad Honnef (Germany): Hoßfeld Verlag 1974

Kant, Immanuel, Kritik der reinen Vernunft, Insel Verlag: Wiesbaden 1956

Kirste, Reinhard et al., publishers, Die Dialogische Kraft des Mystischen, Zimmer-mann Verlag: Balve (Germany) 1998

Nagel, Tilman, Geschichte der islamischen Theologie, C.H. Beck; München 1994

Osman, Fatih, Concepts of the Qur'an - A Topical Reading, MVI Publications: Los Angeles 1997

Rahman, Fazlur, Islam, University of Chicago Press: Chicago 1966

Rumi, Jalal ad-Din, Mathnawi-i ma'nawi, transl. by R. A. Nicholson, 8 Vol., GMS: London 1925-1940

Sekretariat der Deutschen Bischofskonferenz, Christen und Muslims in Deutschland, Bonn 2003

Schimmel, Annemarie, Mystische Dimensionen des Islam, 3rd ed., Diederichs: Munich 1992

Swinburn, Richard, The Existence of God, Clarendon Press: Oxford 1979

Wittgenstein, Ludwig, anthology, edited by Thomas H. Macho, Eugen Diederichs Verlag: Munich 1996

APPENDIX 2
The Concept of Love in Islam
A paper by Barnabas Fund

Introduction: the contrast with Christianity

God's love is the central theme of the New Testament and therefore of the Christian faith. Love is God's main attribute and very essence. The main message of the New Testament is that God is love in His very being, and that this love was revealed in Jesus Christ and His supreme act of love, His self-giving in his sacrificial death on the cross (John 3:16; 1 John 4:7-12).

In Islam, however, the focus is on submission, so love is never more than one of many minor themes. Modern Muslim apologists in the West sometimes assert that God is a God of love. This is not a concept which traditional orthodox Islam would accept, but appears to be a modern stance of adaptation to the environment they find themselves in.

Love in Qur'an and *hadith*

On the rare occasions when love is mentioned in the Qur'an, it is usually in the sense of love between persons and love of material things. Love in the Qur'an mainly means "liking" or "preference". The Qur'an never states that God is love.

There are some verses that speak of humans' love towards God, for example:

> *Yet there are men who take (for worship) others besides Allah as equal (with Allah); they love them as they should love Allah. But those of faith are overflowing in their love for Allah. If only the unrighteous could see behold they would see the penalty that to Allah belongs all power and Allah will strongly enforce the penalty.* (Q 2:165)

A few verses speak of God's love towards specific categories of humans (good Muslims). This love derives from God's will, rather than from His very nature. God loves the righteous by rewarding them, as opposed to the evil-doer who is punished.

> *... verily Allah loves those who act aright.* (Q 3:76)

> *For Allah loves those who do good;* (Q 3:134)

> *And Allah loves those who are firm and steadfast.* (Q 3:146)

> *For Allah loves those who turn to Him constantly and He loves those who*

keep themselves pure and clean. (Q 2:222)

For Allah loves those who are fair (and just). (Q 49:9)

Truly Allah loves those who fight in His Cause in battle array as if they were a solid cemented structure. (Q 61:4)

However, God does not love sinful people and he rejects his enemies.

... He loves not those who reject Faith (Q 30:45)

Verily He loveth not the arrogant. (Q 16:23)

The word most often used in the Qur'an for love is *hub* and its derivatives (*mahabba, yuhibbu,* etc.). This is linked to the Hebrew Old Testament word *ahabah* (root *ahb*) which is the one mostly used to denote love, both God's love to man and man's love to God.

Mahabba, the most common Islamic Arabic term for love, denotes an affection inspired in humans by gratitude for God's blessings. On God's side *mahabba* is usually bestowed as a reward for a good believer who follows Muhammad and submits to God.

Say: If ye do love God, follow me: God will love you and forgive you your sins: For God is Oft- Forgiving, Most Merciful. (Q 3:31)

God's love here for the Muslim who follows Muhammad is a reward rather than a relationship. Early classical interpreters of the Qur'an saw this verse in the light of the polemic against Christians. Christians said they loved God, but as they did not follow Muhammad their claim was wrong. Ibn Kathir in his commentary on this verse says: "This verse is a verdict in the case of anyone who claims to love God but does not follow the way of life laid down by the Prophet Muhammad. His very claim is an absolute lie . . ."*

Love appears also in the other main Islamic source, the *hadith* collections. In the *hadith,* there are references to love for things, love for martyrdom, love for God, and God's love for Muhammad and for deserving Muslims.

---

* Quoted in Sayyid Qutb, In the Shade of the Qur'an, Vol. 2, translated and edited by Adil Salahi and Ashur Shamis, Leicester: The Islamic Foundation, 2000, p. 65.

Love in Islamic theology

According to Islamic teaching, God's essence and nature cannot be known. Therefore a statement like "God is love" (which appears in the Bible, 1 John 4:8,16) would be theologically wrong, even blasphemous, in classical Islam.

Islam does teach that something of God's attributes can be known, and these are described in the form of the "99 Beautiful Names." The names emphasize God's omnipotence and omniscience, his mercy and compassion, his sovereignty and inscrutable will, but not his love.

In Islam God reveals himself mainly through his law (*shari'a*) which calls for submission and obedience. While in Christianity God is personal and establishes personal relationships of love with humans, in classical Islam God is seen as totally self-contained and beyond personal relationships. In Islam, although God loves certain Muslim people of whom he approves, he is not bound to love them even if they deserve his love. Ultimately God is not obliged to do anything, but acts as he wills, sometimes in an entirely capricious manner.

Orthodox classical Islam is more concerned with God's greatness and transcendence, with *shari'a* law and its applications, than with God's love. God is absolutely other, unknowable, far beyond what can be known or imagined (*wara'l wara* i.e. beyond the beyond). The role of humans is to submit, fear and obey God and his law.

For example, following the call in March 2005 by a well-known Islamist scholar, Tariq Ramadan, for a moratorium on the brutal *hudud* punishments still implemented in some Muslim states (amputation, stoning, flogging etc.), several Islamic scholars opposed the suggestion. Sheikh Muhammad al-Shinqiti, director of the Islamic Center of South Plains in Lubbock, Texas, claimed that harshness was part of *shari'a* and any attempt at softening it was giving in to Western Christian concepts which were incompatible with Islam. Shinqiti stated that a personalized faith, like that of Christians, leads to corruption and immorality. He preferred the detachment and severity of Islam, citing the Qur'anic verse

> And let not pity for the twain withhold you from obedience to Allah, if ye believe in Allah and the Last Day. And let a party of believers witness their punishment. (Q 24:2, translation not specified)

In this view, harshness rather than love and mercy are at the heart of Islam. The inference is that Christianity is weak and contemptible because it has love and mercy at its very core.

Love in Sufism

It was left for Islamic mysticism (Sufism) to try to redress the balance and introduce the theme of love into Islam. Sufism offered an escape from the dry and intellectual legalism of the orthodox Islamic teachers and scholars. It focused instead on the human yearning for an authentic personal experience of God. Sufism taught that this experience could be had by a spiritual interpretation of the Qur'an aimed at finding its secret meaning, and by the disciplines of asceticism, repetition of God's names, breath control, meditation and trance.

Rabi'a al-Adawiyya (died 801) introduced the theme of Divine Love into Sufism. She longed to love God only for himself, not for hope of any reward in paradise nor out of fear of judgment and hell. After her death the love theme became a dominant feature of Sufism, expressing the Sufi's endless search for unity with the divine Beloved. The yearning for a love relationship with God was expressed by Sufis in the language of human love, similar to the Bible's Song of Songs and some psalms. Sufi poetry described symbolically the relationship between God the Divine Lover and the human person searching for his love.

Sufis used the Qur'anic verse 85:14 "And He is the Oft-Forgiving, full of loving-kindness [al-wadud]" to express that God loves. From this verse is derived one of the 99 Beautiful Names of God, Al-Wadud (The One who Loves, The Most Loving, The Most Affectionate, The

Beloved). *Wadud,* from the root *wdd,* is somewhat akin to the Old Testament Hebrew word *dod* or *dodim* (plural) used extensively in the Song of Songs for the pure love between man and woman. From it we get the name David (the beloved). However in classical legalistic Islam, *wadud* was interpreted as meaning the one who is favorably disposed, who shows kindness and favor, at most affection, rather than true love.

In addition to the Qur'anic terms *mahabba* and *wudud,* Sufis coined the term '*ishq* for love. '*Ishq* denotes an unquenchable and irresistible desire for union with the Beloved (God).

While Sufism used to be found in every branch of traditional Islam, the legalist orthodox scholars have usually condemned it. Strict Islamist reform movements which have developed in recent times have rejected much of Sufism as pagan additions and innovations which should be purged from Islam. The concept of love is downplayed by such movements and condemned as a pagan, Christian or Western notion incompatible with true Islam.

Glossary

Note: Arabic may be transliterated into English in a variety of ways, so the same Arabic word may be seen with alternative spellings indicating a similar sound e.g. *hudud* and *hudood, Qur'an* and *Koran, da'wa* and *dawah*.

Allah – God. Used by all Muslims and by Arabic-speaking Christians, but with different understandings of the nature and character of God

auliya' – friends, protectors, helpers

dajjal – antichrist

Dar al-Harb – literally "House of War". Classical Islam's term for territory not under Islamic rule

Dar al-Islam – literally "House of Islam" i.e. territory under Islamic rule

da'wa – call or invitation to Islam i.e. Muslim mission

Deobandi – an important Sunni radical movement rooted in nineteenth century India. Deobandis reject folk Islam and Sufi practices and seek to interpret the Qur'an literally. They also reject all Western influence and seek to return to classical Islam. Deobandis form the second largest Muslim movement in Pakistan.

dhikr - literally "remembrance". Meditative repetition of a short phrase, word or part of a word with the aim of achieving a trance-like state of union with God

dhimmi –"protected people". Christians, Jews and Sabeans

under a Muslim government. They were permitted to live and keep their own faith in return for payment of *jiyza* and adherence to various demeaning regulations

fatiha – the first *sura* of the Qur'an, which has a central place in Islam, somewhat like that of the Lord's Prayer in Christianity

fatwa – an authoritative statement on a point of Islamic law

hadd (*plural hudud*) – punishments laid down in the Qur'an or *hadith* for certain specific crimes, and therefore mandatory under Islamic law e.g. amputation for theft, stoning for adultery

halal – permitted by Islamic law (often used of food)

hadith – traditions recording what Muhammad and his earliest followers said and did. Some traditions are considered more authentic and reliable than others

haram – forbidden by Islamic law

hajj – pilgrimage to Mecca

hudud – see *hadd*

irtidad – apostasy, leaving the Islamic faith

ijtihad – literally "effort" or "exertion". A legal procedure used to derive *shari'a* rules for situations which the Qur'an and *hadith* do not cover directly or by direct analogy

Islam – literally "submission" i.e. submission to the will of Allah

Jibrail – Gabriel (the angel)

jihad – literally "striving". The term has a variety of interpretations including (1) spiritual struggle for moral purity (2) trying to correct wrong and support right by voice and actions (3) military war against non-Muslims with the aim of spreading Islam

jinn – a spirit, created by Allah. There are some good *jinn* but many are evil

jizya – poll tax payable by *dhimmi* as a sign of their subjugation to Muslims *julus* – Sufi religious procession

ka'ba – cube shaped shrine at Mecca

kafir (plural *kafirun* or *kuffar*) – infidel i.e. non-Muslim. This is a term of gross insult

kalima – another term for *shahada*

Kharijis – literally "seceders"; a puritanical sect of Islam with a highly developed doctrine of sin. Sinners were considered apostates. The sect began in 657 as a result of disputes over the succession to the caliphate, and continued to rebel against the caliphate for two centuries. They survive today in a more moderate variant, the Ibadis. (Arabic sing. *khariji*, Arabic pl. *khawarij*)

kuffar – see *kafir*

kufr – unbelief (includes apostasy, blasphemy, heresy)

madrassa – Islamic religious school

mahabba – love, the most common Islamic Arabic term for love, denotes an affection inspired in humans by gratitude for God's blessings. On God's side *mahabba* is usually bestowed as a reward for a good believer who follows Muhammad and submits to God

Mahdi – the awaited End-Time deliverer

masjid – mosque

muezzin – one who makes the ritual call to prayer from the minaret or door of a mosque, in order to summon Muslims to pray

mufti – a Sunni scholar who is an interpreter and expounder of *shari'a*, one who is authorized to issue *fatwas*

qunoot – special prayer for times of trouble

Qur'an – the holy book of Islam, comprising a series of "revelations" which Muhammad believed God gave him over the period 610 to 632

rasul – apostle, prophet, messenger

Ruh ul'Amin – literally "the Holy Spirit", used in Islam to mean the angel Gabriel *salam* – peace. A common greeting among Muslims is *as-salamu 'alaikum* meaning "the peace be on you"

salat – ritual prayer, which Muslims must perform five times a day

sawm – fasting

shahada – the Islamic creed: "There is no god but God, and Muhammad is the apostle of God." Also used of the act of reciting the creed in Arabic.

shari'a – literally "the way". Islamic law

Shi'a – the second largest branch of Islam, which broke away from the main body in 657

Sufi – a follower of Islamic mysticism

Sunni – the largest branch of Islam, comprising over 80% of Muslims today. Shi'as and Kharijis broke away from this main body

sura – chapter of the Qur'an

taqiyya – permitted deceit or dissimulation, applicable only in certain situations

tawhid – oneness; the fundamental doctrine of Islam declaring the absolute unity and indivisibility of God

umma – the whole body of Muslims worldwide; the Islamic nation

Wahhabi – member of a puritanical reform movement of Sunni Islam founded in the eighteenth century AD. Wahhabis are dominant in Saudi Arabia

zakat – the obligatory alms due from every Muslim

zikr – see *dhikr*

References and Notes

1   Amir Taheri, "We don't do God, we do Palestine and Iraq," *The Sunday Times,* February 12, 2006

2   For more information on the societal challenge which Islam poses in the West, see (1) *Islam in Britain: The British Muslim Community in February 2005* A report by the Institute for the Study of Islam and Christianity (Pewsey, UK: Isaac Publishing, 2005); (2) Patrick Sookhdeo, *Faith, Power and Territory: A Handbook of British Islam* (Mclean, VA: Isaac Publishing, 2008)

3   Zaki Badawi, *Islam in Britain* (London: Taha Publishers, 1981) p.26

4   Lisa Gardiner, "American Muslim Leader Urges Faithful to Spread Word," *San Ramon Valley (CA) Herald,* July 4, 1998

5   Albrecht Hauser, unpublished lecture, January 23, 2006

6   *Understanding Islam and the Muslims* (The Islamic Affairs Department, The Embassy of Saudi Arabia, Washington DC, 1989)

7   All the sources on Muhammad's life are Muslim and none of them was written earlier than 150 years after his death.

8   *Islam: The Essentials* (Markfield, UK: The Islamic Foundation, 1974)

9   *Understanding Islam and the Muslims* (The Islamic Affairs Department, The Embassy of Saudi Arabia, Washington DC, 1989)

10 The Arabic term *rasul* can be translated apostle, prophet or messenger.

11 Laleh Bakhtiar, *Encyclopedia of Islamic Law: A Compendium of Major Schools* (Chicago, ABC International Group, 1996) p.241

12 Muhammad Taqi-ud-Din Al-Hilali and Muhammad Muhsin Khan, *Interpretation of the Meanings of the Noble Qur'an in the English Language:*

A Summarized Version of At-Tabari, Al-Qurtabi and Ibn Kathir with comments from Sahih Al-Bukhari Summarized in One Volume 15th revised edition (Riyadh: Darussalam, 1996) p.824

13 Abul A'la Mawdudi, *Towards Understanding Islam* (Birmingham: U.K.I.M. Dawah Centre, 1980) p.73

14 As above p.73

15 *Interpretation of the meanings of The Noble Qur'an in the English language* (translated by Al-Hilali and Khan) p.809

16 As above p.47

17 For details of this and the Islamic sources, see Patrick Sookhdeo, *Global Jihad: The Future in the Face of Militant Islam* (McLean, VA: Isaac Publishing, 2007)

18 Khurram Murad, *Shariah: The Way of Justice* (Leicester, The Islamic Foundation 1981) p.6

19 Abul A'la Mawdudi, *Witnesses Unto Mankind* translated by Khurram Murad (Birmingham, U.K.I.M, 1986) pp.2-3

20 "Muslim Brotherhood Strategy for North America: An Explanatory Memorandum on the General Strategic Goal for the Group in North America," http://www.txnd.uscourts.gov/pdf/Notablecases/holyland/07-30-07/0030085.pdf (viewed August 28, 2007)

21 Sura 61, verse 6

22 There are a number of useful works on Islamic spirituality to which the reader is referred for a more detailed survey than is possible here. For example Constance E. Padwick *Muslim Devotions: a Study of Prayer-Manuals in Common Use* (London: SPCK, 1961); Seyyed Hossein Nasr *Islamic Art and Spirituality* (Ipswich: Golgonoosa Press, 1987); Thomas McElwain, a convert to Islam also called Ali Hayder *Spirituality: Christian and Islamic Parallels* (London: BookExtra, 2001).

23 Quoted by Andrew Carey in "Islam's confused identity," *The Church of England Newspaper*, August 28, 2003

24 Charles Moore, "But, Archbishop, this is the bleak mid-winter for many Christians," *The Daily Telegraph*, December 10, 2005

25 Muhammad Taqi-ud-Din Al-Hilali and Muhammad Muhsin Khan *Interpretation of the Meanings of the Noble Qur'an in the English Language: A Summarized Version of At-Tabari, Al-Qurtabi and Ibn*

Kathir with comments from Sahih Al-Bukhari Summarized in One Volume 15th revised edition (Riyadh: Darussalam, 1996). Different translations of the Qur'an can vary slightly in the numbering of the verses. If using another translation it may be necessary to look in the verses preceding or following this reference to find the same text. All quotations from the Qur'an in this book are taken from this widely distributed translation.

26   As above p.47

27   Quoted by Andrew Carey in "Islam's confused identity," *The Church of England Newspaper*, August 28, 2003

28   "British imam praises London Tube bombers," *The Sunday Times*, February 12, 2006

29   Speaking on "A Question of Leadership", Panorama, BBC 1, August 21, 2005

30   Reported by Roz Rothstein and Roberta Seid, "Terror Comes to Georgetown," FrontPageMagazine.com February 22, 2006 http://frontpagemag.com/Articles/ReadArticle.asp?ID=21405 (viewed 24 February 2006)

31   *Islam in Brisbane*, issued by Brisbane City Council (2004), p.3

32   George Archibald, "Textbook on Arabs Removes Blunder," *The Washington Times*, April 16, 2004

33   Sura 2, verse 159

34   Sura 9, verse 30

35   Sahih Al-Bukhari Hadith 3.438, narrated by Jabir bin Abdullah

36   Sahih Al-Bukhari Hadith 4.660, narrated by Aisha and Ibn Abbas

37   http://www.islamonline.net/servlet/Satellite?pagename=IslamOnline-English-Ask_Scholar/FatwaE/FatwaE&cid= 1119503545224 (viewed January 17, 2006)

38   Fahd al-Hushani, "[on the Imam'] Supplication Against Jews, Christians", Al-Jazirah March 10, 2008; translated by Mideastwire

39   "Night Prayer During Ramadhan (Al-Qiyaam or Taraweeh)" issued by Khalid Bin alWalid Mosque, Toronto, Canada http://www.khalidmosque.com/en/modules.php?op=modload&name=Sections&file=index&req=viewarticle&artid=130&page=1 (viewed January 17, 2006)

40   Islam Online – Fatwa, Date of Reply, October 30, 2003 http://www.isla monline.net/servlet/Satellite?pagename=IslamOnline-English-Ask_ Scholar/FatwaE/FatwaE&cid=1119503545224 (viewed January 17, 2006)

41   See for example no. 17 in instructions for "Night Prayer During Ramadan" from the Khalid Bin Al-Walid Mosque, Toronto http://www. khalidmosque.com/en/modules.php?op=modload&name=Sections&file=i ndex&req=viewarticle&artid=130&page=1 (viewed January 17, 2006)

42   "Qunoot - E - Naazilah" http://www.communities.ninemsn.com.au/AM HCY/howtopray.msnw?action=get_message&mview=0&ID_Message=5 92&LastModified=4675414837075584617 (viewed January 17, 2006). Jamiatul Ulama (Kwa Zulu Natal) Council of Muslim Theologians, issued by Al Jamiat Publications, Durban, South Africa http://www. jamiat.org.za/qunoot.html (viewed January 17, 2006)

43   An excellent work on Sufism is P. Lewis, *Pirs, Shrines and Pakistani Islam* (Rawalpindi, Christian Study Centre, 1985)

44   Bill Musk *The Unseen Face of Islam* (Eastbourne, MARC, 1989) pp.229-231

45   As above pp.231-236

46   R. Albert Mohler Jr., "Pope's Comments on Islam Understandable and Clear," On Faith website, November 28, 2007 http://newsweek.washing tonpost.com/onfaith/r_albert_mohler_jr/2006/11/the_pope_the_papacy_ and_the_vi.html (viewed April 29, 2008)

47   Sura 4, verse 171; sura 5, verse 116; sura 3, verse 59

48   Sura 19, verses 34-35; sura 6, verses 101-106; sura 112

49   Sura 19, verse 19. A *hadith* says: "The Prophet said, 'When any human being is born, Satan touches him at both sides of the body with his two fingers, except Jesus, the son of Mary, whom Satan tried to touch, but failed, for he touched the placenta-cover instead.'" (Sahih Al-Bukhari Hadith 4.506, narrated by Abu Huraira)

50   Sura 4, verse 171; sura 33, verse 7

51   Sura 5, verse 110

52   Sura 3, verses 45-47

53   Sura 19, verses 33-34 Muslims interpret these ambiguous verses as a prediction of his second coming, not of his resurrection. See also sura 43, verse 61 which is interpreted in the same way

54   Sura 4, verse 157

55   "That We May Know Each Other; Statement on United Church-Muslim Relations Today" http://www.united-church.ca/files/sales/publications/ 400000126_finalstatement.pdf (viewed April 29, 2008)

56   Philip Yancey, "Hope for Abraham's Sons," *Christianity Today*, November 2004, p.120. It is interesting how the word "ecumenical" has broadened its meaning from "belonging to the entire Christian Church" to include other faiths, especially Islam. Another example of this usage is Peter Kreeft, *Ecumenical Jihad: Ecumenism and the Culture War* (San Francisco: Ignatius Press, 1996).

57   The Organization of the Islamic Conference is an inter-governmental grouping of 57 Muslim states dedicated to promoting the cause of Islam in the world.

58   See Gilbert T. Sewell *Islam and the Textbooks* A report of the American Textbook Council (New York: American Textbook Council, 2003). A recent examination of a draft for the teaching of Islam in state primary schools in the UK, prepared for a regional Standing Advisory Council on Religious Education, revealed similar tendencies.

59   When Muslim school-children are taken to visit churches, they are often allowed a Muslim adviser to accompany them and explain everything to them from an Islamic point of view. It is doubtful whether Christian children going to a mosque would ever be allowed to have a Christian with them to guide their understanding.

60   Tamar Lewin, "Universities Install Footbaths to Benefit Muslim Students, and Not Everyone is Pleased," *The New York Times*, August 7, 2007

61   Jacqueline L. Salmon and Valerie Strauss, "State Dept. Urged to shut Saudi School in Fairfax", *The Washington Post*, October 19, 2007

62   Robin Shulman, "In New York, a Word Starts a Fire," *The Washington Post*, August 24, 2007

63   For a detailed study of the situation of Muslim women living in the West, see Rosemary Sookhdeo, *Secrets Behind the Burqa: Islam, Women and the West* (Pewsey: Isaac Publishing, 2004)

64   See, for example, "Memorandum on Reform of the Islamic Family Laws and the Administration of Justice in Syariah System in Malaysia" (Sisters in Islam, 2000)

65   See for example "Crime or Custom? Violence Against Women in Pakistan,"

Human Rights Watch, 1999. Also Joe Stork, "Human Rights Watch and the Muslim World", *ISIM Newsletter,* March 2, 1999

66   Instructions are given on how long a woman must wait after divorce before marrying again. The ruling is that she must wait for three menstrual cycles, but in the case of a girl who has not yet started menstruation, she must wait three months. Sharia Council "Terms and Conditions for Talak or Divorce" at http://www.darululoomlondon.co.uk/sharia.htm (viewed January 8, 2004)

67   For more examples of *shari'a* councils and *shari'a* courts see *Islam in Britain* (details in note 2) pp. 26-27 or *Faith, Power and Territory* (details in note 2) p. 189.

68   Katherine Kersten, "Shariah in Minnesota?: Radical Muslim activists go fishing in troubled waters," *Wall Street Journal Online*, March 25, 2007 http://www.opinionjournal.com/cc/?id=110009832 (viewed February 12, 2008) ; Barbara Pinto, "Muslim Cab Drivers Refuse to Transport Alcohol, and Dogs" ABC News, January 26, 2007 http://abcnews.go.com/print?id=2827800 (viewed May 1, 2008)

69   OCC Interpretive Letter #806, Dec. 1997, 12 U.S.C. 24 (7); OCC Interpretive Letter #867, Nov. 1999, 12 U.S.C. 24 (7) 12 U.S.C. 29.

70   "Treasury Department Appoints Islamic Finance Adviser", June 2, 2004, Bureau of International Information Programs, US Department of State, http://usinfo.state.gov/xarchives/display.html?p=washfile-englis h&y=2004&m=June&x=20040602180450ndyblehs0.2986959 (viewed October 26, 2007)

71   Christianity is portrayed in the same way in many Muslim-majority contexts.

72   Christians wanting to refer to Muhammad more politely than simply "Muhammad" or to indicate which Muhammad is in question could use the phrase "the Islamic prophet Muhammad" or "Muhammad the prophet of Islam." This avoids implying that his prophethood is valid, as suggested by the media's phrase "the Prophet Muhammad." Another option would be "Muhammad the founder of Islam".

73   Sura 9, verse 29

74   Pnina Werbner, "Stamping the Earth with the Name of Allah: Zikr and the Sacralizing of Space among British Muslims" in Barbara Daly Metcalf (ed.), *Making Muslim Space in North America and Europe* (Berkeley, Los Angeles, London: University of California Press, 1996) pp.167-185. The quote is from p. 167.

75 Any Christians engaging in "prayer walks" in Muslim areas should be aware of this Islamic practice.

76 Sahih Muslim Hadith Book 26, Number 5389, narrated by Abu Harayrah

77 Interviewed by John Ware in "A Question of Leadership", Panorama, BBC 1, August 21, 2005

78 Sahih Al-Bukhari Hadith 5.338, narrated by Ibn Abbas

79 Bassam Tibi, "Blessed are those who are Lied to: Christian–Islamic Dialogue is Based on Deceit – and furthers Western Wishful Thinking," *Die Zeit,* 29 May 29, 2002. Professor Tibi is a Muslim of Syrian origin, now at Goettingen University, Germany.

80 Fatwa # 16642, Islamic Q&A Online with Mufti Ebrahim Desai, April 25, 2008 http://www.askimam.org/fatwa/fatwa.php?askid=33c81b824243 86ffbdcb419a799c578b (viewed April 29, 2008)

81 Martyn Brown, "Outcry as Muslim M&S Worker Refuses to Sell 'Unclean' Bible Book," *The Daily Express,* January 15, 2008

82 *Answers to Common Questions from New Muslims,* collected by Abu Anas Ali ibn Husain Abu Lauz, translated by Jamaal al-Din M. Zarabozo (Ann Arbor, Michigan: Islamic Assembly of North America, 1995) p.27

83 See "Description of Program Content" on the "Three Faiths, One God" website http://www.3faiths1god.com/about.htm (viewed April 30, 2008)

84 Karen Hughes, "Remarks at 'Three Faiths, One God' Film Screening and Discussion," (April 27, 2006) http://www.state.gov/r/us/65326.htm (viewed May 1, 2008)

85 David Gillett, "Banda Aceh – Symbol of our Inter Faith Agenda," *The Reader* Vol. 102, No. 4, Winter 2005, p.8

86 Stephen Lowe, "In a Divided World, the Best Answer is to Unite" in Manchester Diocese's magazine *Crux* , August 2005, p.7. Emphasis in original.

87 Many Muslims consider Ramadan 27 to be the Night of Power but certain groups take other dates in Ramadan.

88 There are many varieties of dialogue including human, discursive and existential.

89 H.M. Baagil, M.D., *Christian Muslim Dialogue* WAMY Studies on Islam 1984 (Riyadh: World Assembly of Muslim Youth, 1984) p.5

90 On January 29, 2008 the Court of Administrative Justice in Cairo, Egypt, rejected a request from Mohammed Higazy, a convert from Islam to Christianity, to have his new religion written on his identity card. The judgment reasoned that, "Monotheistic religions were sent by God in chronological order... As a result, it is unusual to go from the latest religion to the one that preceded it...[a Muslim who opposes this and leaves the religion] is an apostate, manipulating the true religion and leading himself astray." *Sout Alumah*, February 4, 2008 p.6 [Translated from the Arabic]; "Egyptian court rejects Christian's request" Sapa-AFP http://www.iol.co.za/index.php?set_id=1&click_id=68&art_id=nw20080129184432778C629924 (viewed April 30, 2008)

91 Ismail Raji al-Faruqi, *Islam and Other Faiths* (Leicester: The Islamic Foundation, 1998) p. 91: "Evidently, far from being a national state, the Islamic State is a world order in which numerous religious communities, national or transnational, co-exist in peace. It is a universal *Pax Islamica* ... Its constitution is divine law, valid for all ..."

92 To view the full text of The Royal Aal Al-Bayt Institute for Islamic Thought letter from Muslim clerics, "A Common Word Between Us and You" http://www.acommonword.com/index.php?lang=en&page=option1

93 To view the full text of the Yale Center for Faith and Culture response "Loving God and Neighbor Together: A Christian Response to 'A Common Word Between Us and You'" http://www.yale.edu/faith/abou-commonword.htm

94 Michelle Vu, "Christian, Muslim Relief Groups Launch Multi-Million Global Partnership," *The Christian Post*, June 26, 2007 http://www.christianpost.com/pages/print.htm?aid=28165 (viewed April 29, 2008)

95 This is inferred from the fact that the bishop does not mention anything about Christians in Aceh in an article he wrote describing his visit. David Gillett, "Banda Aceh – Symbol of our Inter Faith Agenda" *The Reader* Vol. 102, No. 4 (Winter 2005) pp.7-8

96 International Center for Religion and Diplomacy, "Our Projects / Pakistan" http://www.icrd.org/index.php?option=com_content&task=view&id=83&Itemid=104 (viewed April 30, 2008)

97 Dr. Douglas M. Johnston, "Faith-Based Diplomacy: Bridging the Religious Divide", Remarks to the Secretary's Open Forum, December 8, 2006 http://www.state.gov/s/p/of/proc/79221.htm (viewed April 30, 2008)

98 Jim Landers, "With Coaxing, Pakistan's Religious Schools Shed Militancy," *Dallas Morning News*, March 10, 2008

99 "Wolf Announces New Middle East Initiative," on Congressman Wolf's website, http://wolf.house.gov/index.cfm?sectionid=34&parentid=6&sectiontree=6,34&itemid=70 (viewed May 3, 2008)

100 Rob Moll, "Q&A: Tony Hall," *Christianity Today*, May 16, 2007, http://www.christianitytoday.com/ct/article_print.html?id=45558 (viewed May 1, 2008)

101 To read more about the place of love in Islam turn to pages 146-165 in the Appendix.

102 Teresa Watanabe, "Evangelical Seminary Reaches Out to Muslims," *The Los Angeles Times*, December 6, 2003

103 http://www.fuller.edu/alumni_ae/E-News/2003-12/conflict_resolution.asp (viewed May 1, 2008)

104 http://www.yale.edu/faith/abou-commonword.htm

105 See for example "Christian clerics respond to Muslim hand of peace", Gulfnews.com, November 26, 2007, a report on the Yale Center statement which began with the sentence "More than 300 Christian clergymen signed a letter, apologising to Muslims for Crusades and the consequences of the war on terror, which resulted in human and faith." http://archive.gulfnews.com/articles/07/11/27/10170624.html (viewed April 30, 2008)

106 A particularly good work on evangelizing Muslims is Malcolm Steer, *A Christian's Evangelistic Pocket Guide to Islam* (Fearn, Tain, UK: Christian Focus Publications, 2003).

107 See, for example, Marwan Ibrahim Al-Kaysi, *Morals and Manners in Islam: A Guide to Islamic Adab* (Leicester: The Islamic Foundation, 1996)

108 Letter from Metropolitan Seraphim of the British Orthodox Church to Dr Rowan Williams, Archbishop of Canterbury, February 6, 2006

109 For more information, see Rosemary Sookhdeo, *Why Christian Women Convert to Islam* (McLean VA: Isaac Publishing, 2007).

110 John M. McDermott *The Bible on Human Suffering* (Slough: St Paul Publications, 1990) p.141

Index of Bible References

Genesis 1	22	Ephesians 2:16	101
Deuteronomy 6:5	147	Ephesians 6:12	104
1 Samuel 29:4	101	Galatians 3	
Psalms 116:1,5	147	(especially v.29)	58
Psalms 119:47,97,111	147	Colossians 1:20,22	101
Matthew 5:9	101	1 John 4:7-12	158
Matthew 5:24	101	1 John 4:16	147, 160
Matthew 5:44	9	1 John 4:18	115
Matthew 6:16-18	30	1 John 4:19	152
Matthew 10:16	129	1 John 4:20	148
Matthew 25.40	148	1 John 4	147
Mark 12:30	146	1 John 4:8	160
Mark12:31	148		
John 1:1	22		
John 3:16	22, 95, 116, 158		
John 13:1,34,35	105		
Acts 17:17	86		
Acts 17:22-31	86		
Romans 5:6-11	116		
Romans 5:10	101		
Romans 11:15	101		
1 Corinthians 7:11	101		
2 Corinthians 5:14	9		
2 Corinthians 5:18-20	101		

Index of Qur'an References

Note: Verse numbers vary slightly between different translations of the Qur'an, so it may be necessary to search in the verses just preceding or just following the verse numbers given here to find the relevant text in any given translation.

1 (the fatiha)	72	**3:159**	137, 153
1:6-7	72	**4:36**	151
2:2	87	**4:58**	151
2:159	41 (n33)	**4:114**	151
2:163	150	**4:157**	n54
2:165	150, 158	**4:170**	151
2:169	151	**4:171**	95 (n47, 50)
2:190	24	**4:174**	151
2:222	159	**5:8**	151
2:256	40, 118	**5:32**	40
3:31	137, 154, 159	**5:42**	151
3:32	137,153	**5:51**	76
3:45-47	n52	**5:54**	154
3:59	n47	**5:87**	137, 153
3:76	158	**5:93**	137, 153
3:92	151	**5:110**	n51
3:103	151	**5:116**	n47
3:134	158	**6:74**	136, 150
3:138	151	**6:101-106**	n48
3:146	137, 153, 158	**6:103**	149
3:148	137, 153	**7:26**	151

7:29	151	24:40	150
7:31	137, 151, 153	29:46	87
7:35	151	30:45	159
7:55	137, 153	31:33	151
7:156	150	33:7	n50
7:180	150	35:5	151
8:58	137, 153	35:15	151
9:7	137, 153	40:64	151
9:11	151	42:24	149
9:29	72 (n73)	43:61	n53
9:30	41 (n34)	48:29	151
9:108	137, 153	49:9	159
10:23	151	49:10	151
10:57	151	49:13	151
10:104	151	50:16	149
10:108	151	53:3	151
11:5	149	57:6	149
15:9	87	57:21	150
16:22	150	59:22-24	150
16:23	159	60:8	137, 151, 153
16:51	150	61:4	159
16:90	151	61:6	27 (n21)
16:106	38	63:8	33
17:110	150	64:4	149
19:19	n49	64:6	152
19:33-34	n53	67:13	149
19:34-35	n48	68:34	151
19:96	137, 153	85:14	161
20:8	150	103	151
20:55	151	112	n48
22:5	151	114	151
24:2	161		
24:35	150		

Index of Hadith References

Al-Bukhari 3.438	41 (n35)
Al-Bukhari 4.506	n49
Al-Bukhari 4.660	41 (n36)
Al-Bukhari 5.338	79 (n78)
Sahih Muslim 26.5389	77 (n76)

Index

Aal al-Bayt Institute for Islamic
  Thought, see Royal

Abraham, 22, 58

"Abrahamic" faiths, 58, 98, 115

Abrogation, 39, 53, 119

Abu-Laban, Imam Ahmed, 70

Abu-Zayd, Prof. Nasr Hamid, 68-69

Ad-Din Rumi Jalal, 156

Afghanistan, 10, 50, 65, 72

Africa, North, 3, 45
  Sub-Saharan, 68

Age of ignorance, 32

Agha Khan, 44

Agreements and contracts, 37, 107
  Breaking of, 89
  See also Treaties

Aid and relief, 92-95

Al-Adawiyya, Rab'ia, 161

Al-Azhar University,
  Cairo, and staff, 112

Alcohol, 66-67

Alevis, 44

Al-Faisal, Abdullah, 37

Al-Hushani, Fahd, 42

Ali, Hamid, 37

Allah, 21-22, 37, 54

"*Allahu Akbar*", 21

Alms-giving, 23, 92, 169
  See also dhikr

Al-Qa'eda, 75

Al-Qaradawi, Ysuf, 120

Al-Rekabi, Zein al-Abdeen, 129

Al-Shinqiti, Sheikh Muhammad,
  160-161, 164

America, North, 27, 75

Angels, 22
  See also Gabriel

Anderson, Leith, 121, 132

Anis, Rt Rev. Dr Mouneer Hanna,
  Anglican Bishop in Egypt, 112-113

Antichrist, 22, 106

Anti-Semitism, 60
  See also Jews, Islamic teaching on

Apologetics, 27

Apologizing, 102, 139, 140

Apostasy, from Christianity, 80

   From Islam, 31-32, 62, 68, 69, 74,

   82, 106-107, 108, 126, 141, 167

   See also Converts from Christianity,

     Converts from Islam

Arabia, pre Islamic, 36, 46

Arabic language and superiority, 47

Armageddon, 106

Arts, 39, 96

Assurance of salvation, lack of, 31, 116

Asylum-seekers, 109-110

Atatürk, Mustafa Kemal, 29

Auliya', 76, 166

Australia, 38

   Racial and Religious Tolerance Act

     (2001), 3, 62, 112

   Victoria, 3, 62, 112

Azerbaijan, 44

Badawi, Dr Zaki, 14

Bahrain, 44

Baker, Dwight P., 121

Ball,Hugo, 146

Baptist World Alliance, 128

Barnabas Fund, 118, 122, 136,

   142, 157

Beisner, Barry, Bishop of the

   Episcopal Diocese of Northern

   California, 121

Bertone, Tarcisio, Vatican Secretary of

   State, 123-124

Bible, 95, 133

   Islamic teaching on, 79-80, 87, 123

     on relations with other faiths, 133

   See also index of Bible references

Bin Laden, Osama, 47, 75

Bin Talal, Ghazi bin Muhammad,

   Prince of Jordan, 123

Bishop of Peshawar, 111

Biraderis, 70-71

Birmingham, 75

Blasphemy, 62, 70, 111

   "Blasphemy law" in Pakistan, 68,

     73, 111

Bonaparte, Napoleon, 38

Bourman, Johan, 12-13

Brown, Gordon, 67

Buddhism, 120

Calendar project, 95

CAIR see Council on American

   Islamic Relations

Caliphate and caliphs, 29, 43-45

Canada,

   Toronto, 75

Cartoons, 10, 62, 69-70, 111, 114,

Charities, Islamic, 28

   See also Islamic Relief, Muslim Aid

Champion, Mykhayil Javchak,

   Metropolitan of All America

   Ukranian Autocephalous Orthodox

   Church and Archbishop of New

   York, 126-127

Chane, John, Bishop of the Episcopal Diocese of Washington DC, 81

Chartres, Rt Rev. Richard, Bishop of London, 32, 33, 135

Christian Aid, 93-94

Christian minorities (contemporary), 84, 89, 93, 110
   as scapegoats for actions of the West, 91, 102, 111, 118, 139

Christian-Muslim Forum in England, 81

Christian-Muslim
   relations, 76-113
   Governments and, 11, 97
   See also Cooperation on projects, Dialogue, Reconciliation

Christianity and the Church, 6
   Muslim attitudes to, 8
   Orthodox churches, 13, 107
   Roman Catholic churches, 13, 107, 145

Christianity, failings of historically, 8, 102
   nature of, 143

Christians,
   Arab, 20, 22
   Islamic teaching on, 27, 41-43
   Muslims' relationship with, 76-77
   See also Dhimmi

Church buildings,
   use of by Muslims, 25, 81

Civilizations, 39, 49, 61
   Clash of, 10, 126

Coffey, David, 128

Colonialism, 7, 49, 57, 102, 131

Columbus, Christopher, 38

Community, Islamic
   attitude to, 28
   See also Umma

Compensation, 26, 64, 73, 110

Conquest, 38, 122

Converts from Islam,
   care of, 106, 108-109

Converts to Islam, 90, 100, 115, 136

Cooperation between Christians and Muslims, 91-94

Council of Europe, 70

Council on American Islamic Relations, 15

Creed (Islamic), 23, 30, 55, 83, 133, 168

Crucifixion, 40

Crusades, 7, 57, 102, 138, 139-140

Culture, 2, 3, 16, 29, 39, 48, 49, 58, 65, 68, 101, 103, 128

Cultural Foundation of Abu Dhabi, UEA, 120

Curses, 41-43

Dajjal, 22, 166
   see also Antichrist

Dar al-Harb, 25, 166

Dar al-Islam, 25, 48, 103, 166

Da 'wa, 16, 26-27, 57, 71, 79, 93, 104, 107, 115, 122, 131, 141-142, 144

Deobandi, 96, 166

Defeat, 22, 32, 42

Democracy, see Islam and democracy

Denmark, 69-70

Dervishes, 30

Dhikr, 45, 75, 166

Dhimmi, 39, 72-73, 90, 111, 131, 139, 166

Diakonia, see Service

Dialogue, 32, 85-91, 100, 112, 122, 124

Disasters, natural, 92-95

Discrimination, 110, 111

Dissimulation, see Taqiyya

Divorce, separation and dissolution of marriage, 66

Dogs, 79

Duncan Black Macdonald Center for the Study of Islam and Christian-Muslim Relations, 100

Education, 62-64

Edwards, Joel, 127-128

Egypt, 70, 74, 84, 112

Ekstrom, Bertil, 121

El-Gamal, Mahmoud A, 67

Empires, British, Muslim, 38, 39
See also Colonialism, Conquest

Ephasus, 1st Council of, 148

Ethnicity, 46

Europe, 7

European Union, 70

Evangelical Alliance, 128

Evangelism, see Mission to Muslims

External, importance of in Islam, 30, 39

Fall, the, 55-56

Fallaci, Oriana, 61

Family, Islamic attitude to, 35-36

Fannie Mae, 67

Fasting, 23, 167

Fatimid Empire, 44

Fatiha, 77, 85, 167

Fatwas, 41-42, 66, 79, 167

Fear, 9, 13, 31, 62, 69, 70, 108, 114-115, 122, 160

Female genital mutilation, 64, 65

Finance, 66, 67

Folk Islam, 36, 46

Food, 66, 78

Ford, Prof. David, 128

Forgiveness, Muslim attitude to, 32

France, 61, 141

Freedom of conscience, 31, 40, 114, 143, 145

Freedom of speech, 68-70

Friendship with Muslims, barriers to, 76-77

Frontiers, 121

Fuller Theological Seminary, 98-99, 121

Fundamentalism, Gabriel (Angel), 18, 20, 22, 167

Germany, 70, 79, 141

Gifts, 78-80

Gillett, Rt Rev. David, Bishop of Bolton, 81-82

Global Ministries, 94

God, etymology of,
    Christian understanding of, 52, 54
    image of, 56
    Muslim understanding of, see Allah

Grace, 52, 55, 56, 98

Graves, 41

Green, Lynn, 121

Guardini, Romano, 148

Guilt, 130, 138-140

Gulf states, 50

Guyana, 2

Hadd, see Punishments

Hadith, 21, 25, 38, 53, 69, 76-77, 123, 128, 130, 159-160
    See also Index of hadith references

Hajj, 23, 167
    See also pilgrimage

Halal, 25, 66, 78, 167

Hall, Tony, 97

Hanson, Mark, Bishop, President of the Lutheran World Federation, 127

Haram, 25, 167

Hargey, Dr Taj, 37, 78

Hartford Seminary, 99-100, 121

Hazm, Ibn, 150

Hatred,
    incitement to religious, 61
    See also Australia, Racial and Religious Tolerance Act (2001), Victoria

Hausa, 47

Hauser, Rev. Albrecht, 15

Heaven, 20, 47, 55-56, 69, 116
    See also Paradise

Hell, 22, 36, 106, 115, 161

Hendi, Yahya, 81

Heresy, 57, 74, 166

Hildesheim, Bishop of, 79

Hinduism, 120

Hirsi Ali, Ayaan, 65

History, Muslim attitudes to,
    revision of, 38-39, 63

Hofmann, Dr Murad Wilfried, 136-138, 145

Holy Spirit, 88, 104
    Islamic understanding of, 22

Honour, 32-34, 130
    family, 34, 36, 108

honour killings, 35, 64, 65

Hospitality, 78-80

Houellebecq, Michel, 61

Hub, see mahabba

Hudud, see Punishments Human rights, 142-143,

UN Universal Declaration of, 143

See also Freedom of conscience

Humiliation, 32, 33, 143

Humility, 32, 53, 88, 130, 143, 154

Huntington, Samuel, 10

Hussein, son of Caliph Ali,

Hybels, Bill, 121

Ibadis, 45

ICRD see International Center for
  Religion and Diplomacy

Identity,

Ijtihad, 14, 74, 167
  see also apostasy and kufr

Incarnation, 15, 44, 54, 148

Indian subcontinent, 19, 30, 44, 70

Individualism, 28
  See also Islam, Individuals and

Indonesia, 68, 111, 139
  Aceh, 93, 94-95

Interfaith, see Christian-
  Muslim relations

International Center for Religion and
  Diplomacy, 95-96

International Union for Muslim
  Scholars, 118

Iran, 10, 44, 72, 73, 106

Iraq, 10, 44, 50, 111, 139

Irtidad, see Apostasy

Islam, 39
  anti-America, 3, 43, 107
  anti-homosexual, 3
  anti-Israel, 3, 38, 41 120

anti-West, 7, 47, 50

classical, 14, 24, 40, 64, 72, 96

conservative, 47-48, 78

defending the good name of, 11, 70,
  138-139

definition of, democracy and, 18

diversity of, 8, 43

eschatology of, 22, 106

history of, 33

individuals and, 28, 114, 138

liberals , 48-49, 74

links with Far Left, liberal, 7

loyalty and, 39

militant, 45, 141, 146
  see also Islamism

Nation of, 7

negative aspects of, 38, 68, 143

nature of, 9, 10, 15, 91, 105,
  114, 143

pillars of, 22-23, 25

see also Creed, Prayers, Fasting,
  Alms-giving, Pilgrimage, Jihad

politics and, 9, 24, 28, 70-71, 75,
  115, 116

politicisation of, 48

positive image of, 15, 62

radical, see Islamism revival of, 67

self-criticism and,

spirituality of, 15, 30-31

society and, 28, 110, 142

state and, 28

superiority and, 32, 33, 55, 68, 72, 130, 131

Islamic Center of South Plains, 160

Islamic Relief, 93

Islamic Saudi Academy, 64

Islamic Society of North America, 67, 100

Islamisation,
  of knowledge, 63
  of society, 57, 60, 66, 115
  of territory, see Territory

Islamism, 7, 48, 63, 66

Islamophobia, 7, 16, 60, 63

Isma'ilis, 44

Israel, 25

Italy, 61

IUMS see International Union for Muslim Scholars

Jehovah's Witnesses, 58, 92

Jesus Christ, 52, 104-105, 133
  atoning death of, 55, 95, 116-117, 134
  deity of, 54-55, 122-123, 125, 128, 135
  Second coming, 55, 105-106
  Sonship of, 54, 95, 104
  Christian view of, 54, 135
  Muslim view of, 54-55 123, 128, 133

Jews, 25, 39
  Islamic teaching on, 24, 27, 41-43,

58, 72, 75, 76-77, 87, 120, 137
  See also Dhimmi

Jibrael see Gabriel (Angel)

Jihad, 23, 24, 50, 53, 68, 75, 88, 93, 111, 139, 167

Jinn, 46

Jinnah, Muhammad Ali, 49

Jizya, 72

Jones, Rt Rev. James, Bishop of Liverpool, 84

Jordan, 119

Judaism, 20, 58, 69, 76, 98

Judgment, Day of, 22, 31, 42, 56

Julus, see Processions and walks

July 7th 2005 bombings, 37

Justice, 13, 15, 84, 101, 110-111, 151

Ka'ba, 23, 168

Kafir, 26, 37, 42, 77-78, 137, 168

Kalima see Creed, Islamic

Kamal, Arif, 137-138

Kathir, Ibn, 159

Khalil Gilbran International Academy, 64

Kharijis, 45, 168

Killing, Islamic teaching on, 37

Kuffar, see Kafir

Kufr, 74, 168

Küng, Hans, 101

Kurds, 46

Langham Partnership International, 121

Law, Islamic see Shari'a,

Lebanon, 44

Lee, Peter J., Bishop of Virginia, 121

Left (political) and Far Left, 3

Legal systems and legislation, 61-62
  See also Australia, Racial and
  Religious
  Tolerance Act (2001), Victoria
  See also Shari'a

Livingstone, Greg, 121

London, 75

Love,
  Christian understanding of, 61,
    115, 116, 134, 141, 144,
    145-149, 151-152, 154
  Islamic understanding of, 125,
    136-138, 144, 145, 149-151,
    152-155

Loving one's enemy, 137, 138

Love of one's neighbor, 154

Lowe, Rt Rev. Stephen, Bishop of
  Hulme, 82-83

Lull, Raymond, 117

Lying, see Taqiyya

MacDonald, Duncan Black, 99-100

Madrassa,96, 168

Mahabba 159, 162, 166

Mahdi, 106, 168

Maiden, Peter, 121

Malaysia, 84

Manchester, 75

Marriage, 64, 115

Martyrs, 56

Masjid see mosques

Mattson, Ingrid, 100

Mauritania, 106

McDermott, John M., Mecca, 19,
  53, 58

Media, 37, 68-70
  Muslim, 69
  New York Times, 90
  self censorship, 69, 70

Medina, 19, 53

Metropolitan Airports Commission,
  66-67

Middle East, 46, 97, 140

Minorities, see Christian minorities,
  Muslim minorities

Mission and missiology
  (Christian), Mission, 56-57, 107,
    117, 143
  Islamic, see Da 'wa

Mission to Muslims, 16, 100, 103-106

Misunderstanding of terminology, 18,
  39-41, 52, 88, 104, 144

Mohler, Dr. R. Albert, Jr., President
  of the Southern Baptist Theological
  Seminary, 52

Moore, Charles, 32

Mormons and Mormonism (compared
  with Islam), 20, 58, 92, 149

Moses, 22

Mosques, 83-85, 141

Visits to, by young children, 63

Mouneer, Bishop, see Anis

Mouw, Dr. Richard, Fuller
    President, 98

Muezzin, 59, 168
    see also Prayer, Call to prayer for
    Muslims

Mufti, 79

Muhammad, 41-42, 57, 85,
    129, 168
    life of, 18-21, 53
    veneration of, 19, 30, 46, 53
    compared with Jesus Christ, 19,
        59, 133

Multiculturalism, 2, 7, 60, 92

Murad, Abdul Hakim, 119

Muslim Aid, 94

Muslim American Society, 66

Muslim Brotherhood, 27, 120

Muslim Council of Britain, 77

Muslim Education Centre, Oxford,
    UK, 37

Muslim-majority countries
    (contemporary), 74, 84, 129

Muslim minorities, 39

Muslim World League, 61, 71

Mysticism, Islamic, see Sufism

Mzabis, 45

Nationalism, 49

National Association of Evangelicals
    (NAE), 121

Netherlands, 65

Nigeria, 46-47, 67, 72, 111, 139

Night of Power, 43, 85

Non-Muslims, 26, 37, 53, 63, 67,
    72-73, 77, 88, 94
    Islamic teaching on, 23, 41-42
    See also Kafir

Offa, King of Mercia, 38

Oil, 27

Oman, 45

Operation Mobilization, 121

Organization of the Islamic
    Conference, 62, 70, 71

Orientalism, 69

Overseas Ministries Study Center
    (OMSC), 121

Pakistan, 49, 73, 93, 96, 111-112

Palestine, 25

Palestine Solidarity
    Movement, 38

Paradise, 22, 30-31

Paul, 86, 117

Peace, 101, 102-103, 168

Persecution, see Christian minorities,
    Discrimination

Pictures, 78-79

See also Cartoons Pilgrimage, 23

    Pluralism, 2

Police, 66, 73, 74, 106

Politics, 91

Polygamy, 64, 66

Pontifical Council for Interreligious Dialogue, 124

Pope Benedict XVI, 13, 118, 124

Power, 32-33

Prayer, by Muslims, 23, 41, 83, 85
call to prayer,
for Muslims, 166

Processions and walks, 75, 82, 167

Prophets and prophethood, 54, 58, 122, 134-135

Punishments, for apostasy,106, 108-109, 111
for hudud crimes, 68-69, 71-72, 73, 160

Qatar, 42

Qunoot prayers, 43, 168

Qur'an, 20-21, 53, 69, 80, 87, 95, 168, 118, 123, 128, 129, 130, 133, 137, 158
The Noble Qur'an (transl. Al-Hilali & Khan), 23, 24
See also index of Qur'an references

Racism, 60

Rahner, Karl, 148

Ramadan, 43, 85

Ramadan, Tariq, 120, 160

Rape, 64

Rasul, 168

Reconciliation, 100-103, 122

Regensburg University lecture 2006, 118, 124

Religious liberty, see Freedom of Conscience, Human Rights

Royal Aal al-Bayt Institute for Islamic Thought, 90, 119, 136, 145

Replacement theology, 27-28, 58, 128-129

Revenge, 32, 34

Ruh ul'Amin, 22, 168
see also Holy Spirit

Roosvelt, Theodore, 13

Sacranie, Sir Iqbal, 77-78

Sacred space, 75
See also Territory

St Francis of Assisi, 154

St John of the Cross, 152

St Theresa of Avila, 152

Saints, Muslim, 46

salam, 167 see also peace

salat, 167

Salvation, 52, 56, 134

Samir, Samir Khalil, 125-126

Satan, 22, 106

Saudi Arabia, 50, 64, 68, 70, 84, 106

sawm, see fasting

Schools, see Education, Science, 39, 96

Secularism, 6, 58, 95

September 11th 2001 attacks, 10

Seraphim, Metropolitan, Bishop of Glastonbury, 112-113

Shahada see Creed, Islamic
Shakespeare, William, 39

Shame, 34

Shari 'a, 16, 25-26, 39-40, 55, 56, 62, 65-67, 71, 75, 78, 102, 111, 125, 120, 169

Schools of, 74

Shari 'a councils and courts, 65, 66

Shari 'a compliant mortagages, 66, 67

Shi'a Muslims, 30, 38, 44-45, 69

Sin, original 55-56

Slavery, 28

abolition of slave trade, 7, 92

Somalia and Somalis, 65, 72

South Africa, 79

Sri Lanka, 94

Submission, 39, 72, 114, 181

Sudan, 67, 72, 74, 106, 139

Sufism, 30, 45, 75, 136-137, 61-162

Sunni Muslims, 38, 44, 46, 96, 112, 169

sura, 169

Switzerland, 61

Taha, Mahmoud Muhammad, 69

Taheri, Amir, 2

Taliban, 65, 72

Taqiyya, 37-41, 52, 88-89, 144, 169

Christian, 90

Tauran, Cardinal Jean-Louis, 124

Tawhid, 122, 144, 169

Territory, 9, 25, 75, 83

Testimony (in law court), 26, 64, 73, 110

Theology,

Christian viewpoint, 142

Islamic viewpoint, 145

Tolerance, 62, 72, 86, 88, 91, 96, 114, 123, 129, 144, 154

Treaties, 102

See also Agreements and contracts

Tribes, 58

Trinity, the 54, 104, 123, 125, 134

Troll, Christian W, 124-125

Truth, 82, 83, 115

Tunnicliffe, Geoff, 121

Turkey and Turks, 29, 45, 46, 111

UMCOR see United Methodist Committee on Relief

Umma, 26, 28-29, 32, 43, 77, 93, 169

United Arab Emirates, 79

United Bank of Kuwait, 67

United Church of Canada (General Council), 57

United Kingdom, 2-3, 66, 67, 70, 75, 81-83, 95, 108, 112, 141

London Borough of Tower Hamlets, 75

United Methodist Committee on Relief, 94

United Nations, 62, 70

Universal Declaration of Human Rights, 107

United States, 7, 11, 27, 65, 66-67, 78, 90, 97-100, 121, 126, 141

Connecticut, Hartford Seminary, 97-100

Fairfax, Virginia, 64

Foreign policy, 107

Georgetown University, Washington DC

Lubbock, Texas, 161

Minneapolis-St.Paul airport, 66

New York, 64, 75

Office of Comptroller of the Currency Administrator of National Banks, 67

State department 64, 81, 97

Treasury Department, 67

See also Islam, anti- America

University of Michigan-Dearborn, 63

Uthman, Caliph, 20

Van Gogh, Theo, 70

Vatican, The, 123

Verwer, George, 121

Violence, 61, 102, 111, 116

Volf, Dr. Miroslav, 120

Wahhabism, 44, 46, 96, 169

Walks, see Processions and walks

War, 126, 130, 138, 140

See also Jihad

"War on terrorism", 10, 40, 102, 138, 140

Warren, Rick, 121

Warsaw Declaration (May 2005), 60

Western society, 6-7, 50, 60, 61, 72

Wilberforce, William, 92

Williams, Most Rev. Dr Rowan, Archbishop of Canterbury, 7, 127, 128

Willow Creek, 121

Winter, Tim, see Murad

Witnesses, 73

Wittgenstein, Ludwig, 149

Woodberry, J. Dudley, 121

Women in Islam, 34, 36, 53, 64, 70 oppression of 39, 64-65

World Assembly of Muslim Youth, 87

World Council of Churches, 11

World Evangelical Alliance, 121

Worship, Christians joining in Muslim worship, 81, 85

Muslims leading Christian worship, 80, 81, 82-83

Visiting each other's places of worship, 80

Wright, Christopher J H, 121

Wright, Henry B., 120

Yale Center for Faith and Culture, Yale Divinity School, 90, 102, 120

Yale College, 99

Yemen, 44, 46

Yoruba, 47

Youth With A Mission (YWAM), 121

Zakat, see Alms-giving Zikr, see Dhikr

Zwemer, Samuel M, 99